For Mom and Dad

Frank Kern

In Search of the Perfect Onion Ring

A Son's Stories of Life, Death, Cancer & His Dad

By Chris Kern

Open Door Publications

In Search of the Perfect Onion Ring
A Son's Stories of Life,
Death, Cancer & His Dad
By Chris Kern

ISBN: 978-0-9981208-2-9

Memories have their own truth, and this book reflects only my own memories and recollections of events and people. I've included only first names, to respect people's privacy, and of course, some of the dialogue is recreated. I hope that anyone mentioned here will enjoy my memories of them.

Cover Design by Genevieve LaVO Cosdon, LaVODesign.com

Photos of the author by Jason Reese, Photorexit Photography info@photorexit.com

Printed in the United States

Published by
Open Door Publications
2113 Stackhouse Dr.
Yardley, PA 19067
www.OpenDoorPublications.com

Table of Contents

Frantically a man flailed
Water splashed
He called to those nearby and to those he could not see
Life vests and buoys were thrown, without success
No boats could be found
Without options, rescuers retreated
Desperately fighting, arms waving,
his head bobbed above and below the water
He gasped for air
Still pleading and flailing
the tired man slid under the surface

Diagnosis

I met my dad at the doctor's office near his home. It was a cold winter day. I had no idea of the road that lay ahead for both of us. I wondered why the heck he'd asked me to be there. Dad was quite capable of going to the doctor alone. He was mobile and in good health. He drove there. He walked in. He filled out his paperwork himself.

The first sign of Dad getting sick had been just a few days after Christmas. We spent Christmas Day together hanging out at my house (his old house, which I had bought from him and Mom when they moved to a smaller apartment). We ate, watched TV, and exchanged gifts. While quiet, it was a good day.

My sister had warned me of his yellow skin tone. Dad had a neighbor, Gretchen, who was in her 90s. My sister told me that Gretchen told Dad his color looked just fine. I met Gretchen many times in the months to come. She was a very nice, friendly woman who Dad helped with delivering her mail. Gretchen must have been color-blind, because that day at the doctor's office, the Dad I was looking at was the color of a yellow legal pad.

✦✦✦

I was fortunate to know Trudie. We met while we were both salespeople for a wholesale plant nursery in Iowa. I saw her mostly at trade shows. She introduced me to some good nursery people, and was always very helpful.

She and I became friends and did a fair number of partnership business deals together over a few years. Trudie never let me down. We never had to write even a penny's worth of credit for any deal we did together. We talked often about availabilities, prices, shipping, and such. Trudie had pancreatic cancer and passed away not too long prior to my dad's diagnosis. Even during some of her sickest moments she would talk to me on the phone. She promised things would get done, and they always did.

I didn't know anything about pancreatic cancer prior to hearing Trudie's diagnosis. I remember being on my upstairs porch, speaking to a friend on the phone about her. A quick Google inquiry opened my eyes to this killer. I recalled the five-year survival rate was about five percent, and one-year rates were not much higher.

When my dad was diagnosed in late December 2011, I knew he had been given a death sentence. I did the math in my head. I would not travel for work that summer.

I spoke with Trudie's son, James, who had taken over her accounts. I asked about her illness, and what to expect with my dad. He talked freely. I felt for him. I feared for my dad. I feared for me.

✦✦✦

There are lots of tough guys in the world. I had one friend who worked a summer on an Alaskan fishing boat. His uncle owned a fleet of them, but he could not tell anyone for fear of being singled out. He hated it. Fish, fish, fish, then go to port and watch all his tough guy shipmates pick fights at the bar. Another friend Jeff was a Marine who, upon discharge, did some very deep undercover work, so secretive he couldn't even tell you who he was working for, let alone what he was doing. With only one finger, he could drop you to your knees and make you beg to be released.

Dad was not a tough guy. He headed in the opposite direction from confrontation. It's not that he let people walk all over him. He ran companies. He sat on local boards. There must have been conflict, and he must have handled it well, because there was very little turnover in the organizations he ran. He handled most issues in a manner much more dignified than I would have. I tend to be mouthy, direct, and go against the grain. I was probably good practice for Dad.

Once, I saw my dad stand up for himself. It wasn't just for himself, but for the entire Kern family. I witnessed the short exchange. I was shocked. It was not like my dad. There was no backing down. No hesitation. No question in his mind. He knew he was firmly in the right. He was a gentleman. Someone drew a line in the sand, and Dad walked right up to it and took one step over it.

Fuck You, Asswipe.

Those would have been my words, but I never got the chance. Dad's way was much more dignified.

✦✦✦

I know an MMA (Mixed Martial Arts) fighter. Drank beer with him more than once. My son Clint is friends with him. I would not want to get on his bad side in a fight. Dad was not a person who would step into a Mixed Martial Arts cage match and come out a winner. Dad's strength came from deep within, an unwavering rock solid foundation of strength. It is a strength that only comes from faith. But time and time again I witnessed his strength. Time and time again others told me of his strength.

✧✧✧

In the last few years, after Dad retired and Mom was gone, he called pretty much every day, and often stopped by unannounced when in the area. I was usually "busy," and would make myself take a breath, get off the phone with a customer, or stop what "important" thing I was doing to spend a few moments with Dad. His unannounced visits annoyed me.

A year or two before he got sick we fell into the routine of having dinner together about once a week. Maybe a little more. We usually spent an hour or maybe two together, which was plenty for both of us! I was glad to have dinner with Dad and I enjoyed our time together. With that said, though, when I get a rare headache it is stress related. I feel horrible saying it now, but I would usually leave Dad with a headache, and have to take a couple of aspirin chased with a beer. Sometimes I just went ahead and took them before dinner. Dad may well have done the same.

✧✧✧

Dad had gotten forgetful. I laugh at it now but time after time *this* was one of the headache creating events. He had a funny habit of telling the same story over and over. Dad and I would be eating dinner, and he would start to tell a story. About a minute into it he would pause to ask, “Have I told you this before?” I would answer “yes.” Almost as if deaf Dad would not react and just continue on with the story as if never having asked the question. He did this every time we were together, sometimes more than once. It became pretty funny once I began to anticipate it. In my mind I was shaking my head back and forth and saying “really,” with a sarcastic smile on my face that said, “You are seriously doing this again?”

It pretty much never stopped, but after Dad got sick I became more appreciative of his stories, realizing someday they would stop and I better enjoy them while I could.

What I wouldn’t give right now to spend an evening listening to my dad tell me the same story over and over a few times.

The year or two before Dad got sick, I occasionally sent my sister, Beth texts with a short, funny story about my dinner with Dad. She lived far away and did not see him often. In my mind, I wanted her to be prepared as I saw Alzheimer's in Dad's future. I didn't want her saying she had no idea and why didn't I say something. So, I sent a funny story here and there, usually related to some brain fart he was having. They were never mean-spirited, just funny old Dad stories. Beth enjoyed these stories and would often call after a text to follow up or laugh with me.

For these few years, Dad and I generally had quiet birthdays, Thanksgivings, and Christmases together. Since my divorce, Mom's passing, my three boys growing up, moving away, and having other places to be, things had changed for Dad and me.

At Christmas, Dad usually gave me a gift of a nice check, and maybe a small item he picked up. Buying my 80-year-old dad gifts was not easy. I usually gave him a book, maybe some clothes he didn't need, and a random stupid item I'd see at the store that never got used. He had grown to like feeding birds, so he could always use fifty pounds of sunflower seeds. I had to stop buying him different types of new birdfeeders because I learned that if I got him a new birdfeeder, soon the (completely fine) old feeder would show up at my house destined for my yard. He really didn't want MORE feeders.

The last Christmas we were together I handed him a card with $200 worth of restaurant gift cards. As I handed it to him I said, "I know I always give you these, but I kind of enjoy spending time with you." He opened the card then handed me a card saying, "I feel the same way!"

I opened my card, which also contained various restaurant gift cards!

✧✧✧

I tend to find way too many things that I can do tomorrow. Why get in a hurry? Why get stressed? Do it tomorrow. It's not going anywhere...or is it?

The closer to home it is, the more I tend to put it off. Forty-seven years ago, Dad moved back to Evansville with Mom, my sister, and I to become the Executive Director of the Evansville Association for the Blind, a sheltered workshop for the visually impaired and handicapped. Over the years, I watched the transformation of the EAB under his direction as it grew and grew and grew until the most recent expansion. Now the building covers the entire city block. It was so big in its heyday Kmart purchased over a million dollars' worth of mops from them; they also assembled parts, did packaging, and other normal and odd jobs for Whirlpool, Berry Plastics, Inland Container and other local and national companies.

I was understandably impressed, as were others I know, when the last big expansion was named to honor my father. There on the new brick building were the letters, "Evansville Association for the Blind FRANK E. KERN BUILDING" standing out in white.

Glen, a close friend, asked if I had a photo of Dad standing in front of the building. I said no, but I would get one. Years and years went by, and I never got the photo. The building was going nowhere. Neither was Dad.

As I sat in the hospital with my dad knowing his condition, it bothered me for days, really bothered me. That building kept crossing my mind. As luck would have it, Dad was released late one afternoon. We pulled out of the hospital, located a few blocks from the EAB, onto Virginia Street. I headed west toward Dad's and, as we approached the building without driving one inch out of our way, I pulled over and said, "Let's get a photo of you and your building."

The late afternoon sun perfectly lit the side of the building. Dad posed for his photo without protest. He was probably wondering what took me so long!

✦ ✦ ✦

Chris Kern

I've always been amazed at the lack of protest from loved ones when taking photos toward the end of their lives. I think they know these could likely be some of the last photos of them. Sitting at the kitchen table, or in the recliner, lying in hospital beds wearing hospital gowns, sporting unmade hair, sitting in wheelchairs, all the family gathers around and, if possible, they hand the sick person the baby to hold. We were fortunate to have months to take photos with Dad. There are lots of smiling faces, and no shortage of smiles from Dad himself.

✧✧✧

On the way to St. Louis, Missouri, Dad wanted to stop at Missionary Oblates of Mary, just across the border in Belleville, Illinois, to see a retired priest who long ago had been helpful to Dad.

Dad had helped set up a radio reading service for the blind in the Evansville area. This priest had done the same in his area, and shared his experiences with Dad. When we arrived, Dad did his thing: asked questions and tracked the priest down on the large grounds. The retired priest was busy with a group of mostly wheelchair-bound residents all circled around playing some kind of fishing game. Each had a pole and was trying to "catch" fish on the floor.

The priest, who was also in a wheelchair, was wheeled into the hall. Dad explained who he was and why he was there. Probably forty years had passed since the 90-plus-year-old priest last saw my father. I stood off to the side after meeting the priest, and tried not to interfere. After some conversation, the priest recalled those earlier years and the help he offered. I was touched by Dad's sincere appreciation of the priest's contribution years before. The visit did not last very long. The priest wanted to return to his game and his friends. He called Dad and I together before we left and offered a prayer.

About three weeks after finding out Dad had pancreatic cancer, we went to St. Louis, Missouri, for a second opinion from a specialist surgeon. It is an easy three-hour drive from Evansville to St. Louis. We decided to catch a St. Louis Blues hockey game. We arrived in St. Louis early and parked at Union Station, a few blocks from the arena. We walked around Union Station and grabbed a bite to eat. We went up to the hotel and sat in the lobby. I had a beer. Norah Jones music was playing. The architecture was outstanding. Dad slept in a lounge chair. The peacefulness made it easy to surrender and forget what brought us here.

Close to game time we picked up our tickets at Will Call and headed to our seats. I wanted to get great seats because I figured this would be the last pro hockey game Dad ever saw. We had center ice seats about six rows off the ice. Because Dad was so close to the ice, I could tell he was having difficulty following the puck. We usually sat up higher at our local hockey games where, I did not realize until that moment, he could follow the puck more easily. I watched the crowd above us slowly file in. Two young guys were sitting in aisle seats about twenty rows above us. On my way to the concessions I pointed out our seats, explained Dad was having difficulty seeing the puck, and asked if they would consider trading seats after the first period. They looked at me like I was nuts and said sure! We ended up in their seats, and Dad was much happier.

After the game the crowd was moving fast, and Dad was moving slow. I did my best to block and protect him with my body. It was cold, which was hard on him. In just walking those few blocks I could see how much he had declined physically in the past few years. I had never noticed it before.

The next day the surgeon asked Dad if he was capable of walking up three flights of stairs and Dad said yes. He probably could, but not brisk, and not twice. Surgery was going to be harder on him than I suspected only a few days before.

The New Normal

When I was growing up, Dad was always open about where he kept important papers, such as insurance and financial records. Just in case something happened we would know where to look for them. I never paid much attention, except maybe to know a general direction to look should the need arise. About three years before he passed, when Dad was around 80, he took me to the bank and added me to the signature card as joint owner on his checking and savings accounts, and his safety deposit box. I didn't give it much thought, except now my name appeared on the checks he wrote me for my birthday and Christmas presents. I did not have to access the monies, safety deposit box, or even sign a check for years.

When Dad left the hospital in early January 2012, it all changed.

"It's all fine that I know where you keep your records," I announced, "but that's not going to work for me. We are going to pick a dresser in your apartment and put everything in one place."

We cleaned out the proper size drawer, and that's what we did. As we assembled the paperwork, Dad talked as I paged through the stacks of documents. I asked questions while making mental notes. Bad idea. There was information overload, stress, and too much time before revisiting the papers. I wish I had added Post-it notes on the paperwork as necessary. This was my big opportunity to ask freely what I needed to know while Dad was willing and able to answer all my questions. Not realizing it, I let a lot of important information pass by me.

I have known families whose loved ones will not talk, plan, or otherwise deal with death. I feel for them. I have seen large sums of money lost, businesses sold, and long-held lands parted with to pay the tax man, because of lack of tax planning. On the other end of the scale, I watched from the fringe a family business that is large enough to go public. They constantly plan so the business may continue after the owner's passing. In my opinion, it is complicated and requires way too much effort and money on their part. This is time and money that could be better spent by them growing their business, hiring more people, or simply passing it to the next generation. While I did not have inheritance and tax issues, even a small estate has transfer of ownership issues, and the simple act of adding my name to Dad's checking, savings, and safety deposit boxes made life that much easier.

I am lucky I have just one sibling, and that we get along reasonably well. Having a death and family dynamic issues on top of that would be a nightmare. Fortunately, Beth and I generally see eye to eye in the whole scheme of things.

There was a point when openness and willingness to discuss financial matters disappeared. I can't remember exactly when it happened, but it did. As Dad inched closer to death, his inclination to discuss matters I would have to attend to after his death lessened, and then stopped. Eventually, I felt these matters were off-limits and stopped trying to get help from him.

I feel fortunate Mom preplanned the funeral, cemetery, headstone, and such. I feel fortunate Dad wrapped up 99 percent of the paperwork after her death. There were a few insignificant matters that surfaced when I had to show Mom's death certificate to prove her passing so her assets could transfer to Dad, and to Dad's estate, and eventually to myself and Beth. I feel fortunate Dad planned and kept generally good records. I feel fortunate he was willing to be open and discuss his financial life with me.

✦✦✦

I ventured out to the patio I built the year before. It was a beautiful sunny, early summer afternoon. I called Dad and said, "The Otters are playing tonight."

"I saw that," he replied.

The Otters are our local minor league baseball team. It's owned by Dad's attorney, Bill, who we often spoke to at the games. Dad usually sat with the booster club in a reserved seat sporting his name. He was more reserved than some of the members. I think he enjoyed their antics.

Dad said he would need a wheelchair. I told him I'd thought of that.

He said he could not make it the entire game and would have to leave early. I told him I thought of that, too.

I was happy because I did not expect him to be up for going to a game that year. I dropped him off near the entrance, parked, and returned to him. The Evansville Otters play on Bosse Field, the third-oldest ballpark in the country still in use professionally. It is where parts of the movie *A League of Their Own* was filmed. It is a beautiful old park, and I love the atmosphere. I pushed Dad in, past the booster club members who all said hi. We got a good spot on the rail and watched some baseball. Later I learned Bill came over to say hi and catch up with Dad just as we headed to the bathroom. He figured he would say hi later. Unfortunately, we never returned to the game. With Dad in a wheelchair, Bill offered us his parking spot. We never got a chance to use it.

✦✦✦

For many years, Dad had University of Evansville basketball season tickets. Eventually, he let those go when he moved to the west side. He started to frequent the University of Southern Indiana games, and seldom went to the UE games. He sat just behind the USI bench and got to know the coaches and players. More than once over the years the basketball coach stopped by to say hi to Dad when he saw him out at local restaurants. Dad tutored some of the players, too. It was kind of funny that Dad was not a ballplayer, but he was always part of the game.

On two occasions when Dad was sick, my friend Calista offered me her seats to the UE game. I took Dad. It was a good time, and I had not been to a game in many years. Dad enjoyed it, and we managed to get to the seats without going up too many steps. Steps...who knew steps would become such a big freaking deal?

Before each game, we visited a nearby Italian restaurant. Before she died, Mom used to always talk to the owner. They must have hit it off because she got away with murder there. She once got me a last-minute reservation on Valentine's Day. They put up a folding table for me and my date, and just made room for us. Any time Mom did not see the owner upon entering the restaurant, she simply walked back into the kitchen to find him. You would have thought she owned the place!

When we went to the restaurant before the first game the owner was heading out the front door, and we caught up in the street. He talked with Dad for some time, then helped us up the steps, and got us settled in our seats. That was the last time they talked.

✧✧✧

For the first few months of Dad's sickness you really couldn't tell he was sick. He acted and looked as he always had. And the people around him acted normal to him, too. I saw him a little more frequently than in the past, but not abnormally so. Even after starting to see Dad every day he seemed pretty much normal. But there was a point when his cancer started to take its toll on him faster than he could keep up. It was a gradual attack.

I would notice something about Dad that was different. A new need, a new way of doing something, a new request, whatever. He may have needed me to help him do something today. The next few days he would be back to himself. Then he might ask for help again. Then he was okay by himself. The next time he asked I might have to help him on two days instead of one.

As I began to notice this pattern, it became obvious what was going on. I came to realize whatever he did new today would be the "new normal" within about two weeks. If he used a cane today for the first time, in two weeks he would use a cane every day. If he needed help with laundry today, in two weeks he would always need help with his laundry. The progression went this way with everything in his life. Cane, walker, wheelchair. Those were noticeable. I found that two-week pattern an interesting progression. Once I noticed the pattern, I was able to ease my mind into what was coming next. That was helpful, too.

✧✧✧

Dad always had a list. I don't remember him being such a list maker before getting sick. Mom was the list maker, not Dad. Now, he would scribble who called on envelopes, what they spoke about, appointments he need to make, or go to. He had lists showing the time he took pills. We were always trying to get more calories in him, so he kept a list of what he ate. When going through Dad's stuff after he passed away, I found a list of restaurants. Places we went or should go. I kept that list.

Dad kept a list of when he took his medications. It was confusing as he had lots to keep track of. There were a few occasions I think he goofed up, maybe taking double of something by mistake. There were a few times he was pretty loopy. Cancer sickness, general weakness, mistaken meds...who knows.

One night he was particularly loopy. I wondered if he had taken double meds. I could have talked to him about it, but why? I had mixed feelings. I wanted Dad around as long as possible. I wanted him pain-free. I didn't want harm to come to him. But the clear reality was soon he would not be with us. I pondered for a moment what would be more tragic for him—lying in bed beat up by cancer, slowly dying, and knocked out with morphine, or his screwing up his meds one night and just never waking up.

I could keep a reasonable eye on what was happening, but I could not be there 24/7. He didn't need that, and he surely did not want that. How could I keep him from taking his meds, and a few hours later forgetting and taking them all over again? I couldn't, and the outcome in the long run would be of little difference. Enjoy today. Let tomorrow take care of itself. Ultimately, we were blessed, and an excessively painful end for Dad did not materialize. His pain management seemed "easy" compared to some of the stories I'd heard.

✧✧✧

For months Dad and his doctors chased after the cause of the pain in his upper leg. It caused him to shift positions often, and lose sleep. I don't know how much his cancer pain medications masked the pain in his leg. I never saw Dad in agony with his leg. It was, however, enough of an annoyance that he had multiple discussions with doctors, x-rays, and scans done to try to identify the source of the pain. Nothing definitive was ever determined.

As Dad lost weight his feet somehow got larger. They swelled to the point at which wearing his regular shoes became impossible. He wore house slippers with a solid sole everywhere. They made a clopping sound. The time came when they needed to be replaced. Dad and I went to our local Kohl's, and he tried on every house slipper they had. Nothing worked. Nothing felt right to him.

Kohl's was very empty the evening we stopped in. At the register was Chris, who lived next door to Cousin Harold's house. She had spoken to Dad a number of times over the years. I had also met her on occasion. After some friendly chit chat, she suggested Dad try a pair of Crocs. I could not imagine my dad wearing an ugly, holey, trendy pair of plastic shoes, but he tried them on, and they fit his needs perfectly. He loved them!

I had a dilemma. I am neither a trend setter or follower; I'm more a trend avoider. I saw the Crocs trend had come and stayed. My dad was about to purchase Crocs. In my mind, there was no way I could allow my 83-year-old Dad to get a pair Crocs before me. Dad and I got our first pair of Crocs together.

Dad wore those Crocs every day and everywhere. Dress slacks and Crocs—what a combination! I still wear mine daily, though mostly as slippers. I have the original black pair and now a camo pair I got for my lake property, where I live full-time now.

One afternoon my dog, Kain, and I arrived while Dad was napping. I could see Dad in his chair, so we fed the birds and swept the patio before entering the apartment. At my direction, Kain nudged Dad's arm, and Dad awoke startled. This rude awakening was met with protest by Dad and a scolding aimed at me. To this day, I still feel bad about my decision to let Kain awaken Dad. Six months prior Dad would have woken with a smile, a pat, and talked to Kain. Not this time.

Dad was tired, on medication, stressed, and not pleased with me. There were other times he wanted things done his way and he may have been short with me if I varied from his direction. Nothing memorable, though. He never flew off the cuff. He did not yell, cuss, or belittle. I wrote off any shortness to his sickness, medication, and stress. It's much easier to let things bounce off your shoulder when you realize it's not you, but simply your loved one not feeling well and you just happen to be in front of him at the time.

✧ ✧ ✧

In Search of the Perfect Onion Ring

Looking back there were lasts. Sometimes you know a last and sometimes you don't. At the time, I had no clue what would be the last restaurant meal we would eat together. I know now. I knew at the time the last pro hockey game we would see together was the one we saw in St. Louis soon after Dad became ill. But the possibility of Dad passing did not go through my brain 24/7, and because of that, stupid things happened. Sometimes I was just in normal mode and didn't shop for him as if it was a last. Other times it was in the forefront of my mind.

One day he asked me to pick up tacos to eat in his apartment. Taco Bell immediately popped in my mind. I drove to the west side of town, and as I approached the Taco Bell restaurant it hit me. "I'm not buying Dad Taco Bell for his last taco meal!" I headed over to a little local Mexican place we frequented. I'm still surprised that it didn't occur to me sooner. Those were far from his last tacos, but it might have been!

Another time he asked me to pick up toilet paper. Then a few days later he asked to buy him toilet paper...again. The second time I put a little thought into the purchase and did not just grab the first package I saw on sale.

One of the coolest "last" things I saw him do was order lobster tails one evening. He didn't want a salad, steak, potato, rice, or veggie. Nope, keep all that stuff. Can I just get two of those little lobster tails and some coffee?

✦ ✦ ✦

Summer in Indiana brings strawberries. One evening we were parked near the carryout entrance at a local BBQ place. A huge sign promoting their strawberry pie hung by the door.

Dad said, "Bring me some of the pie."

When Dad opened the container at home it was without a doubt the nastiest looking (and tasting, I presume, because Dad did not eat but a bite) pie I have ever seen. Lucky for Dad shortly afterwards we went to a church Sunday dinner where he got a proper piece of strawberry pie. (I recently went past that BBQ place and noticed it is out of business!)

In what had been Evansville's busy business district where Dad spent his childhood, a gentleman had opened or revived three restaurants within a few blocks. One is a popular German-themed place in an old hardware store. Another one is a pool bar with great onion rings. The newest is an Italian restaurant with a huge improvement in offerings over its previous menu. While the main dishes were great, Dad was disappointed with the antipasta salad he ordered. I'm assuming his disappointment was that it was not prepared as traditionally as he desired. It sticks with me because I could almost see on his face he knew it was the last one he would ever have, and it was just not right.

You want to fix it. You can't. It's just a freaking salad. But it's his last freaking antipasta salad, and suddenly it matters. It mattered to me anyway.

✦✦✦

At first Dad and I did not spend time every day together. As the months went by, the days per week we spent together increased. Eventually, we did see each other every day; we grew into that routine. As we spent more time together we ate out more often. I would say we were eating out three or four evenings a week, and as much as I may try to eat reasonably, it was not always on my plate!

Dad would order his meal, and I would order mine. After some time, my bathroom scale reflected my eating decisions and the frequency of our outings. One day when Dad and I got together I started to open my mouth to say, "Dad, we've got to cut back on these dinners because I'm gaining too much weight."

Literally, a fraction of a second before I spoke, out of his mouth came, "I'm glad we go out to eat, because I probably would not eat any dinner otherwise."

Wow! That was unexpected. I immediately realized dinner was an important part of keeping Dad going. If that were the case I was on board a hundred percent!

To make it more fun for me I decided to try to find the best hand-battered onion rings a restaurant could deep fry for our eating pleasure. We split an order of onion rings anytime we could find them made in-house. Each was different, but damn homemade onion rings are the best even on a bad day.

Dad ate a little more food when we got those onion rings. I decided to worry about my weight later. I found keeping Dad eating enough calories was a creative effort and a losing battle.

✦✦✦

It wasn't really the onion rings that were important. I like them. I should not eat them every day. Freshly made rings are not uncommon, but only say five percent of restaurants have them so they are not as easy to stumble across as, say, a handmade patty burger. I enjoy it when I find really tasty ones fresh out of the deep fryer. I prefer the thinner cut rings, rather than the thick ones. Thinner ones can be greasy, but the thicker ones hold the batter better. And a place with really good freshly made onion rings usually has a pretty good burger, too.

Some of the best onion rings I ever had I think were a mistake. I think they got done too early and were set to the side. When it was time to serve them they had to be put back on the grill to warm them, which resulted in grill marks and a bit of grill flavor. They were the thick type. I thought they were great! Never had them before or after, even at the same place.

But my search for the perfect onion ring wasn't really about finding the "Holy Grail of Onion Rings." The onion ring was secondary. It was the journey, not the destination, that was the focus.

I like seeing roadside attractions when I travel: the odd, weird stuff along the highways. I also enjoy the interesting architecture in the small downtowns I pass through while on the way to the attraction, and the little mom and pop restaurants, or the 99-cent taco stand outside the gas station in a small Tennessee town.

If you didn't look for the attraction you wouldn't have found the taco stand.

The search for the perfect onion ring has nothing to do with rings. It has to do with attitude. It has to do with the journey. It has to do with what you find along the way.

I gave this little thought at the time. I just knew I like fresh rings. I knew they were not everywhere. I knew I was going to be eating with dad...a lot. I knew I was going to put on more weight so, what the hell, I might as well be eating what I liked and not be like a girl before bikini season all worried about it and shit! Eventually, I knew he needed more calories. Eventually, I saw he ate more than usual when we got rings. Rings were a bonus.

✦✦✦

Dad and I met our friend Big Larry many of times for dinner. Big Larry is Dad's age. They used to hang out as couples, but both had lost their spouses. I went to school with Big Larry's kids, and worked after school in his pharmacy. Big Larry is not big, but has a son named Larry, so it became Larry and Big Larry.

We would often meet Big Larry at the Hilltop, a popular, very old, local west side tavern. Big Larry eats fast, and doesn't linger long to socialize after dinner. He used to sit in our living room and read the newspaper during my mom's parties. She HATED that! He was always trying to improve his golf swing. He is pretty laid back, and I can't say I ever saw him lose his temper. I've always thought quite a lot of Big Larry. I came to respect him greatly and thus asked him to be in my wedding. My high school and college friends plus Big Larry stood up for me. When Dad turned 80, my sister put on a big birthday party for him.

Now, my wife is my ex-wife, but three of my groomsmen were still there for me and my dad, including Big Larry.

✦✦✦

By now Dad and I were eating dinner together regularly every day. I got a phone call from my friend Gregg. Gregg's parents and mine were also longtime friends. He and his brother were my fraternity brothers, and I knew his sister in college, too. He called to tell me his parents had asked Dad out to dinner. Dad declined and told them he would have lunch with them instead. Gregg went on to explain Dad had told his parents in the evenings he had dinner with me, and we ran errands together.

I think Gregg wanted me to know this because Dad had chosen our daily outings over a friend's dinner invitation. Gregg thought that spoke volumes to what Dad thought of us spending our evenings together. There had been a hump to get over for both Dad and me. We went from spending some time together to spending every evening together. One hour with Dad in the past often gave me a headache. Now I spent entire evenings with him, often under much more stressful circumstances, and never got a headache.

✦✦✦

I don't know how we did it, but $35 seemed to be the number. It became a joke between us. One day I told him I noticed no matter what we did, we spent about $35 when we went out. We ordered the two-for-whatever special when we first started eating dinner together. That was a good value.

Later, when Dad did not order his own meal, we lost the value the special offered, so while we got less food, we often paid more. But somehow, if we ate very cheap one day, I'd need some gas...$35! Even if we decided to cook at my house, I still went to the grocery store to pick up a few items. I would throw in some ice cream, maybe some wine...the total would be around $35. I even showed Dad a grocery receipt once because I thought it so strange. If we had tried, we would never had been successful at spending $35. But randomly we succeeded.

Dad quit paying for things months before his passing. I asked him several times if he had a dollar or two when I was short on tip money. He just didn't have cash in his wallet. He didn't need it. So, for months I paid. I wasn't worried enough to lose sleep about it, but at the time I was not flush with cash. Logically, I should have not been eating out every night, and certainly not with a guest and paying for us both, but logic was off the table at that point. It was just time to spend with Dad, and I could worry about the details later.

Beth knew of our $35 evenings. It was that funny to Dad and me that others knew about it, too. After Dad's passing Beth and I were discussing some financial matters concerning Dad's accounts. She brought up the meals and asked me to put a dollar figure on it all. I told her I felt uncomfortable doing that. She did some figuring on her end of the phone and suggested an amount to cover my extra spending over that time. She was generous with her figures. She could have nickel and dimed the amount but she didn't. She told me to take that amount off the top when settling Dad's financial matters and pay myself back. I was grateful to be able to knock down my credit card balance.

After several months Dad still did not seem *that* sick to me. We were spending lots of time together, but I guess I was not a hundred percent comfortable with that, yet. One day Dad and I had plans for dinner when my son Josh called and asked if he and his girlfriend, Devon, could join us. I told him yes, but suggested I bow out to let them spend the time with Dad, as I was seeing him every day. I thought it would be nice for the kids to spend one-on-one time with Grandpa. But I also had a selfish motive. I enjoy cooking and had not done much of it lately. I wanted to cook some salmon on the grill. Josh's call gave me an opportunity to enjoy an evening alone cooking, while allowing the kids and Grandpa some personal time. A win-win. Josh still remembers running around with Grandpa that evening, just like Grandpa and I would have done. Grandpa made his planned stops. I think they had a good outing.

I cooked a nice meal, as I had planned, and was happy to have an evening off to do as I pleased...or so I thought. While it was good to have the kids spend time with Dad, I had an uneasy feeling. While I don't remember the exact day, I do know until the day Dad died, I never again went without seeing him every day, including the day I personally had to prepare for a medical procedure. That time I saw Dad in the morning, and again the next day when I was not allowed to drive, I still picked up a late dinner and had carryout with Dad that evening at his place. I risked driving myself to him, but did not risk driving him around. Looking back, I needed that day off to realize I wanted and needed to see him daily. I made a conscious decision to spend a part of every day with Dad, no matter what. That decision made my life easier, and my time with him more enjoyable.

✦✦✦

Dad asking for ice cream got me on an ice cream kick. He could usually eat an entire single serving container, so I stocked up on a variety when shopping. I started with the common flavors, and tried to throw in a few new ones. For both Dad and me, simple works. We know what we like. No need to mix it up too much. He could have eaten vanilla or chocolate every day and been very happy.

I found that out after when I brought him Cookies and Cream. He threw it out after a few bites and went back to old-fashioned vanilla. I liked that he enjoyed it, and I knew he was getting much-needed calories.

The whole time I was trying to get calories into Dad, he was wrestling with diabetes. He was trying to listen to his doctors, and while I was trying to be respectful of that, in my mind I was balancing things: calories/weight loss/cancer/diabetes.

Without calories we could not fight the others. I put diabetes way down the scale of concerns. Quality of life, pain management, and perhaps other things came before blood sugar. Not to be cavalier about it, but I figured if he had a serious fatal complication from diabetes, it would be more of a blessing than a curse for him.

✧✧✧

In an effort to increase calories, the doctors suggested Dad drink Ensure. I made numerous trips to WalMart and CVS for Ensure and Boost. I stood in the store reading the labels, comparing brands, and getting over the fact this was now our lives. I tried mixing it up by getting different flavors. After a while we got the right mix of three or four. Some went faster than others, so I adjusted the quantities. I could usually find some other treats he liked. Power bars did not go over well. Some nuts did. I tried anything with calories.

Dad did his part. He liked Wendy's Frosties, and asked me to bring him one out every now and then. I brought him a small, but that was still too big for him to finish. It took a try or two, but whatever he ate was still extra calories.

✦ ✦ ✦

There is a little restaurant in a nearby town known for its catfish, or fiddlers as they are called here. I've never been the biggest catfish fan, but Dad loved them. He would always order catfish, and I would get a half chicken, white meat. When ordering, I would tell the waitress to bring me a box, too because I would save half the chicken I ordered for the next day's lunch. We also got an order of onion rings, stacked high and tasty! We ate there every so often when Dad was in the mood for a short twenty-minute drive.

For most of that year Dad could get around, albeit slowly. He had to consciously watch his steps and actions, but he was still mobile. I liked eating in the bar area, which required a step up or down, depending on your direction of travel, and opening a western saloon style door. If Dad needed to visit the bathroom, off he went.

One night, a high school-aged waiter was heading toward the bar area and saw Dad heading his way. Like a good employee, he made the decision to hold the door for him before realizing just how slow and labored Dad's walking was. The kid was now stuck waiting patiently for this old man to make it to the doorway and take a step into the other room. Dad made his way to the restroom and back.

Later, when the young waiter headed into the other dining room, I announced to Dad I now had to go to the restroom. What I really wanted to do was talk to the young man. Unfortunately for him, and for me, the kid was headed to the restroom. My mind was focused on speaking with him and without thought, I followed him in.

He took his spot, and I followed the unwritten guy rule and took my spot as far from him as possible. Another unwritten guy rule is you pretty much never talk to a stranger in the restroom unless maybe you're at a sporting event and the place is jam packed and everyone is joking about the smells, sounds, or officiating. So, in the quiet small restroom I did the unthinkable...I spoke. I can only imagine what was going on in his head, and I'm sure he was trying to figure how the hell to make his exit ASAP. Talking to the wall, I explained what a nice gesture it was for him to hold the door open for my dad. I explained it may have meant nothing to him but it was a huge thing for my dad. I told him it made his trip much easier. Eventually, I could tell the kid relaxed and was listening to me and not worried about my being a threat to him. He knew I was sincere and that he made someone's life a little easier that day.

As I watched Dad's condition worsen, and every movement take more effort and thought, I wanted to make sure this kid realized his seemingly small gesture of kindness was a big deal to me and so helpful to this slow old man. By holding the door open patiently for an awkwardly long time, he helped an old, sickly person easily navigate the opening. It doesn't take much to make the world a better place.

When I was younger I used to look for the "big thing" to do in work, life, whatever. I was probably an ass and usually miserable back then. Now, for lots of reasons I just look for what I can do right now with what I have. Hold open the door, be friendly, smile, let a car go first, let someone know they are thought about, give a friend a hard time to make them laugh...whatever.

Several times Dad and I ended up at The Pub to eat. I love hamburgers. Good burgers, bad burgers, thick, thin, whatever. I love burgers. The Pub makes a great burger. Thick, juicy, topped with cheddar, bacon, and some grilled onions...heaven. Oh, and did I mention they make a mean onion ring, too?

We ate there at least twice while Dad was sick. The first time was late April or early May. The air-conditioning was running already, and Dad was cold. We asked our waitress if she could find a jacket, maybe from the lost and found box, to help us out. She did find a random jacket hanging on a coat rack, and Dad was very happy. This interaction led to a conversation about Dad's health and his illness. Dad opened right up, while I was worried he should not. Once again, I was shown things happen for reasons beyond our ability to comprehend. It turned out that day our waitress had just found out a loved one had a serious cancer. She was at a loss with many questions and concerns.

Dad made her feel so welcome, she literally sat at our table with us at for half the time we were there. While that might be a nightmare in some cases, it was not in this case. She was a person in need, and Dad connected with her in his way. It worked for them.

In late May we returned on my birthday for more burgers and onion rings. The waitress was not able to take care of us that evening, but she stopped by to talk. Things were not going as well with her loved one. Dad's condition had also worsened. He was losing weight, and it was very noticeable.

I went to T he Pub in July to relax, clear my head, and get a burger. I sat alone in the booth. A waitress I didn't know, but who obviously recognized me, came over to ask how my dad was doing. I told her he was near death. It was nice she remembered him.

✦ ✦ ✦

Doctors

Dad had some amazing doctors. Some I would enjoy drinking a beer with and getting to know better. Others, not so much. One of the doctors who was in the first category was a smart Eastern European lady. I would have enjoyed talking more about her native lands. I like that kind of stuff.

His first surgeon, the one who placed the stents, knew his stuff. He took the necessary time for us. I could tell he loved what he was doing. This may not be a fair description, but I always had the feeling it was more about him and his ability to fix Dad than it was about Dad. It was pretty cool when he took me back to the operating area to show me on the video monitors what he had done during Dad's surgery. He was good. He loved his work.

Dad's oncologist set us up with an appointment in St. Louis with a bigwig surgeon to get a second opinion. I figured Dad was too old, too weak, too something to be a candidate for major pancreatic surgery. But I also figured this was a step we had to take in order to cross off possibilities so we knew we had done all we could.

I got a hotel close to the doctor's office in St. Louis. We filled out all the check-in paperwork, and I don't remember what else. I do remember being in a very small exam room for some time before the doctor came in. When he did arrive, the room was crowded with interns, too. There were five to eight of us crammed in this closet-sized room.

The surgeon had reviewed Dad's file. He determined Dad was a candidate for surgery—which surprised both Dad and me.

The doctor took out a binder, like what you would expect from a replacement window salesman, and started paging through diagrams of body parts and telling us what he could do. Dad interrupted to ask a question, and the doctor stopped him. No questions allowed during his presentation. Questions were only allowed when he was finished paging through his book. He made it clear this was his show, and he was running it his way. During our visit, the doctor had an emergency case requiring his immediate attention. He was on the phone several times during our visit. Understandably, his attention was divided.

The end result: The odds of beating pancreatic cancer via

surgery were around 30 percent.

Because we lived three hours away, the doctor's office had set other appointments for x-rays and tests the same day we saw the doctor. It was for our convenience. But...

I remember being in that little room while the doctor gave Dad two minutes to decide whether or not he wanted to have surgery. Two minutes. He even said it out loud. "I'll be back in two minutes."

I had directions to the other hospital in my hand. I can see it in my mind along the interstate, but for the life of me I don't remember if we went there or not. What I do remember is being somewhere along the interstate in Illinois and Dad asking me if I thought the trip was a waste of time. Somewhere between leaving the doctor's office and that stretch of interstate in Illinois, he decided not to have that radical surgery.

I may have been thinking to myself just what Dad asked, and I may have been thinking it was a waste of time. I also think he made the right decision, that it was the decision he should have made, and it was the decision I wanted him to make. You try to run every scenario through your mind. What would be the best action for the best outcome? In the end, I told Dad it was his decision and to remember everyone he asked for their opinion would have their own agenda. I said that because I knew my agenda was somewhat based on Trudie's struggle following the same surgery. I was as fearful of him having the surgery as I was of him not having it.

When we got back to Evansville, we met with Dad's oncologist. Long story short, Dad asked him if he made the wrong decision.

The doctor looked at Dad, and then looked at me, and said to me, "If you said no, I would put you in the car and drive you back over to St. Louis myself...you are only 50."

Then he looked at Dad and explained he had already beaten the odds living longer than his average life expectancy, had a good quality of life, it was a very complicated surgery, with a long difficult recovery, and he was surprised the surgeon was willing to do the surgery. He explained that a "successful" surgery is measured differently by different people. I think he was letting us know, based on his conversations and interactions with Dad, he agreed this was the best decision.

I wonder if the surgeon had had a warmer bedside manner if Dad would have made a different decision. I wonder. I can say their personalities did not complement each other. I didn't care for his bedside manner myself. I will say this: If someone had to operate on Dad, I was convinced that surgeon had the knowledge, skill, and confidence to carry it off successfully. I am sure he would have been the right man for the job, and my dad's best chance for a successful outcome.

✦ ✦ ✦

Dad and his oncologist got along pretty well. As I look back writing these stories I wonder how much Dad's personality brought out the best in other people.

I have witnessed too many odd interactions not to believe Dad just brought out something in a stranger. Conversations often centered around Notre Dame sports, football in particular, but it could have been religion, or common acquaintances, or a service group. Dad usually made some connection with people.

Very often on his visits with his oncologist I had to say, "Dad, the doctor has other patients to see. We've got to go and let him work."

The two of them would just talk and talk, and I don't really think the doctor was too worried about it. Never once in all the visits can I remember Dad's oncologist ever rushing Dad along. Not even a hint. When you were with him, you couldn't help but feel you were his only patient. His only reason for being at the office. His only concern.

You knew he had many patients. You knew he was juggling between patients and the nursing staff was there assisting him, but when it came time for him to give you his complete attention, that is exactly what you got. You would have thought you were the only person there for him to see.

Dad found a doctor who struck a balance between treatment and quality of life. He and Dad were a good fit, and that alone led to a better quality of life for Dad.

✦✦✦

Dad had a toothache. His regular dentist was on vacation, so he saw the dentist covering for him. He suggested Dad make an appointment with an oral surgeon. He explained the appointment would be weeks in the future. I spoke privately to the dentist, explaining Dad's health. Once he understood weeks were like years to Dad, he was able to be fit right away into the oral surgeon's schedule with an appointment early one afternoon.

After an examination by the oral surgeon, it was decided to do nothing. I suspect this had to be a borderline call based on his experience. What would deteriorate faster? The tooth or Dad's overall health? I called Brad, a close dentist friend of mine, to ponder the possible outcomes. I think the surgeon made the correct decision. He made it clear he would make room for Dad if his condition worsened. Ultimately, it came down to Dad's short life expectancy and the high doses of pain medications he was already on.

After the exam was over, Dad and the doctor chatted for over twenty minutes about Notre Dame football, Dad's work in Georgia, and whatever else. Just chatting like old friends, even though they only met a few minutes earlier.

I thought he was finished for the day and was heading out for a round of golf with friends. That's really what I thought. The whole time I'm thinking he has some time to kill before his tee time, so he's just being nice. When he opened the exam room door to let us out, two nurses were standing there with charts to hand him and tense, frantic looks on their faces. I could tell that twenty-minute conversation had totally ruined those nurses' afternoons and now all his appointments would run late. He must have been truly interested and enjoying his conversation with Dad.

✦✦✦

In the hospital, right outside the entrance where Dad received his chemotherapy treatments, was an eye doctor's office. It had a storefront with large counters and lots of frames on display. Dad needed his frames adjusted, so after chemo he walked in and started talking with the girls. He got them to adjust his glasses, asked if they knew the eye doctors who had been on his board of directors, and just generally started to make friends. All the girls came over to help. By the time we left they were offering to make any needed adjustments in the future. Total bill for their time...zip! I told Dad if he kept this up I might even end up with a date.

Dad got a postcard from his longtime eye doctor's office reminding him of his need for a yearly eye exam. Dad was a rule follower. At this point, Dad's health was in noticeable decline. His mobility was limited. You could see the end was sooner than you might want to consider. The card floated around his kitchen but he never threw it away as I hoped he might. Finally, one day he announced he needed to go for his annual eye checkup. He may have even made the appointment, I don't remember. Sometime in the conversation that followed I simply asked did he really want to mess with it. I had been thinking of it and in my mind, I couldn't justify the difficulty of taking him for an eye appointment, the discovery he would need a new prescription, the possibility of needing new frames, waiting for the new prescription to arrive, going back to get the new glasses, and getting everything adjusted all while realizing in a month or two he might be gone anyway.

I hated to think that way, but this one just didn't add up. Dad did not get an eye exam. It was the right choice. I doubt he was negatively affected by not getting new glasses.

✦✦✦

For a number of years I have been trying to become better at being proactive with my own health. I have a nice, younger doctor whom I like very much, and I try to keep a schedule of regular checkups. He spends the time necessary and always tries to encourage me to do things I'm not going to do, such as cut back on salt, drink less, and exercise more.

He also has a spiritual side, and I'm okay with that. I happened to have an appointment with him during the time Dad was sick. We talked about Dad's pancreatic cancer. Knowing a bit about the doctor, I asked him to remember my dad in his prayers. He said he would as we both exited the room. Then he stopped in the hall, handed my file to a nurse to hold, and pulled me back into the exam room. To my surprise, without hesitation or preparation, he gave the most heartfelt prayer for my dad's treatment and comfort.

Harold

Harold was Dad's 93-year-old cousin. Dad was his personal representative. Harold was in and out of a nursing home because he kept falling and not getting up. Other than that, he was, in my opinion, a reasonably healthy 93-year-old man. Turns out Harold had more money than most people would have imagined.

Harold hated being in the nursing home, but refused to allow staff in his home to properly care for him. Dad was in a Catch-22 situation and was frustrated about it. Dad could have updated the home for Harold and staff and arranged for 24-hour care. There were sufficient funds, and this could have continued for years. But Harold would not have it. Harold refused in-home care. He would fall, finally be found, go to the hospital, go to the nursing home, recover, go home...only to do it all again months later. Toward the end the nursing home stays got longer, then they became permanent.

Harold never gave up on going home. I don't think many folks do. Weeks before his death, he was still talking about going home. I think there are many empty homes in many cities around the country just being held onto because no one wants to take away hope. Years can go by, all the relatives know their loved one is never going home, but the home remains as is. Strangely, it's probably best for all involved.

Several times I ran stacks of personal mail and magazines to Harold's room at the nursing home. I cannot say it was the most enjoyable activity I have ever done. As nursing homes go, I would not have wanted to be there. It was very close to Harold's home; that was why it was originally picked. Harold's room was small and included a roommate. Noticeably on Harold's side of the room was a small TV with the volume uncomfortably high, and always tuned to the Catholic channel. Between my hearing not being so great, Harold's age, and way too much background noise, conversation was difficult. I did the best I could.

Dad would also visit when he could. It wasn't much easier for him toward the end for the same reasons. We would stay, but I could tell Dad became increasingly uncomfortable as his condition worsened. Visits became very short. The toll on Dad became increasingly noticeable.

We visited Harold again just before his death. Harold was sleeping, and heavily medicated. His breathing was labored. It was not pretty. We left quickly. I remember Dad was in his wheelchair, so his condition had noticeably declined. I knew Dad had made his last visit to the nursing home. He was always a gentleman, but I knew he couldn't get out of there fast enough. My mom would have said, "offer it up," and I'm sure he never said a word about the visit and his feelings, but he had to be "offering it up" because he knew he was not far behind. That had to be hard on him. I can't say I ever initiated a visit at the nursing home with Dad. I went on my own several times, but when I went with Dad it was because he wanted to visit Harold. This last time I am very glad I did not initiate the visit. I would have felt terrible.

Harold passed away a few days later.

✧ ✧ ✧

Tim was Harold's longtime attorney, whom I finally met around the time of Harold's death. I remember talking with Tim at the church before Harold's funeral. He had hurt his leg and it was in a large cast which made getting around a challenge. We knew Harold's time was near, and Jerry, the funeral director, and a longtime family friend and neighbor, asked Dad to gather some military information about Harold and find one of his suits for the funeral. By chance that was the day before Harold passed. That evening Dad and I went to Harold's home and, as Dad sat in a chair in the living room, I looked for the requested items and information.

After quite a search I found a file of papers outlining his military career. I also found his only suit, a 1970s style leisure suit. I planned to run it by the dry cleaners the next morning and get it looking sharp.

But that was the morning Harold passed. There was no time for the dry cleaners, so I ran by the funeral home to speak with Jerry. I dropped off the file with additional notes about Harold for the obituary. Then I asked about the suit. Can you help? Simple, Jerry replied...$168 for a suit, tie, and shirt. Perfect, I told him. Do it!

At the church, I commented to Tim that Harold would be rolling over in his grave because I spent $168 on his suit. Harold looked good. He deserved it! At 93, you have outlived most of your friends, and Harold was kind of his own guy anyway. He never married. He had his way of doing things. He was a HAM radio enthusiast who regularly spoke with people around the world. Harold was a loner. His funeral was quiet. There was a handful of people who knew Harold, a few others who came out of obligation. I guess that's why Dad and I stayed there all afternoon. Most of the time we were the only ones there with Harold.

✧✧✧

The funeral Mass was lightly attended, too. Jerry made sure, as he did for every funeral, that there were enough able-bodied pallbearers.

Harold had preplanned and purchased a spot in a mausoleum. He'd picked a premium spot, just inside the main entrance and about four or five spots up. It seemed like an uncharacteristic splurge.

Harold had a military funeral. A few family members attended, with Dad being his closest relative. We sat in the front row. This was my second military funeral. My first was only the year before. They are impressive and respectful of those who have served. It's an honor to have one and an honor to attend one. For whatever reason after the flag was folded in the traditional triangle shape, it was presented to me. I respectfully listened to the words recited to me about the lost comrade and said "thank you" when he placed the flag in my hands. Dad and I both knew the flag was destined to be with one of Harold's nieces or nephews who attended the funeral. Afterwards I passed the flag to one of them.

Dad never wanted a military funeral. He said no when in the past I specifically asked him about it. Dad always spoke fondly of his military years. He was part of the occupation forces in Germany after World War II. On one snowy day at the Baumholder Army Base he was speaking to a superior who asked if he could type. Dad could, and was told, "then you will type." Dad protested he did not want to type, at which point the superior pointed out the window to the parade ground where snow was falling and troops were marching. He gave Dad a choice. "You can type or march." Dad typed.

Harold had passed away recently. Being busy with funeral arrangements and the like, Dad and I were not in our regular routine of errands and dinner. Dad usually put some thought into the activities of the evening. Often, we picked a restaurant in the general direction of the planned activity, and filled in the blanks from there. This evening one of the blanks was checking Harold's mailbox. I usually also threw in a quick walk around the outside of his house.

I pulled in the drive, got out, and gathered the mail. Because Dad was with me, I handed the stack to him to go through. I hopped back in the truck and drove up the driveway turn-around. As Dad sat in the truck sifting the mail, I did my quick walk around the home. We had not been to the house since the day before Harold passed away. For whatever reason that evening I decided to open the door to the breezeway and check the garage and kitchen doors. I did this maybe once in ten trips, maybe even less often.

I walked in and quickly noticed the kitchen door wide open. I looked inside and saw a giant Big Gulp soda cup on the kitchen table. I decided to go back out to the truck. Meanwhile, Dad was going through the stack of mail in the truck. I handed him my phone and showed him how to unlock it and make a call.

"Someone's been in the house. If I don't come out, or someone else comes out, call 911," I told him.

I went back to the kitchen door. All was quiet. Just inside the door were two new Craftsman tool chests. Within the past year Harold had asked Dad to purchase them for him. I was drafted to deliver the units, and Harold insisted on assembling them without help. The empty cardboard cartons were still in a pile in the garage. Harold intended to keep some of his camera equipment in the cabinets.

Having been through the house only the week earlier looking for his military records, I knew the cabinets held cameras, lenses, filters, and other camera equipment. It also held medical receipts, various owner's manuals, copies of check stubs, empty pill bottles, and assorted random items. Oh, and the tool chests also held a few tools.

I grabbed a ball peen hammer from the top drawer, and for good measure added a sturdy, if well-used, utility knife. I walked straight into the house through the kitchen, past the bathroom and the closed basement door to the back bedrooms. I could tell they had been rummaged through, so I backed out of the house, only stopping once again at the Craftsman cabinets. I opened the drawers with the camera equipment and they, too, had been rummaged. The cameras, lenses, and macro equipment were all missing.

Meth labs are a serious concern in our city, and so the thought of someone using Harold's house to cook meth crossed my mind. I decided it wouldn't be wise to venture into the basement.

✧✧✧

Back at the car I called the police, and soon a sheriff's unit pulled up. I told him our story and walked around the home with him. He decided to call for backup. When the other officer arrived, they both entered and investigated.

After they cleared the home they asked me to do a walk-through with them. We went through the house room by room discussing what had been moved or was missing. They dismissed someone breaking in for drugs as too many pill bottles remained in the home and several bowls of loose coins remained untouched.

There was not much in the living room other than furniture and books so I had not gone there earlier. It was only as a second thought we entered it this time. What I found strange was that a huge pile of photo negatives that had been on a folding card table the week before were now missing. Harold was a lifelong photographer and spent countless hours organizing his negatives. I had looked at them briefly only the week before. He had taken my parents' wedding photographs. He took the picture of my grandfather that hung in my room for many years while growing up. Dad also found a photograph of my grandfather I had never seen before. That's why I remembered the negatives. I wondered how many other photos of my grandfather were hiding there.

Just prior to his death, Harold had a number of photos published in a book about the local zoo. While I could not be certain, I suspected next to no one would be interested in those negatives, with the possible exception of another photographer who might recognize their possible historic value (which would equal the odds of winning the lottery) or a family member who wanted them for their sentimental value. After discussing the situation with the sheriff deputy, he phoned a family member from Chicago who had also been at the funeral. He left a rather firm message and his phone number.

This entire process took several hours, with Dad sitting in the car the entire time. You could tell just sitting and waiting with all the activity around him had taken a stressful toll. He was weak; this did not help at all.

We were back at his apartment getting him settled when

the family member called back. He had spoken with the deputy. It seems between the end of the funeral, and before lunch and him leaving town, some of the other family members "not me," he said, had decided to "lay claim" to the missing items. He was sure, however, they locked the doors when they left. He was sure they did not leave the empty Big Gulp soda cup on the kitchen table either.

We changed the locks. The attorney representing Harold's estate fired off a terse letter to the rest of the family. The other family members did not want to make an issue of the items that had been removed, so the matter was dropped. I was once again shown how odd people act when someone passes away.

I was more pissed at the unnecessary amount of stress Dad went through over this occurrence. His health was already failing rapidly. It was as if this experience took weeks off his energy level. Yes, it was uncalled for and unnecessarily stressful.

✧✧✧

The Last Summer

When I was a sophomore at the University of Evansville, I attended a school in England they owned called Harlaxton Manor. It is a beautiful manor house built by Gregory Gregory near Grantham, England, 110 miles north of London. My room was in the stables, which are grander from the outside than most homes one sees in a lifetime.

The months I spent at Harlaxton and in England changed and forever molded my life. At Harlaxton I met a pretty and interesting girl, whom I became fond of, named Beatrice. She was from Germany. Her dad was German, and her mom was French. Both became U.S. citizens. Her father was a Sergeant in the U.S. Air Force and was working at Rhamstein Air Force Base.

When school was out my roommate, Carl, and I traveled for three weeks around Europe. Since Bea and I had been dating, we put her home on our itinerary. After four months in Europe we missed the States greatly. Bea stocked up with American treats from the PX. American chips and candy and such. What a treat! We were close to two American bases and made trips to them to go to the cinema. During my time away from the United States, I had grown to love it even more, and understand it was the greatest country on earth. Before the movies started, everyone stood up and the national anthem played. Since then, it is my favorite part of a sporting event.

✧ ✧ ✧

Once, as we walked around the base, I had a strange feeling I had been there before, yet that was impossible. The feeling was very strong and unexplainable. Weeks later when I returned home and sat with Dad, I told him about my travels and being on the Rhamstein and Baumholder bases. He quietly stood up and pulled a cigar box out of the closet. As he thumbed through the photos I stopped him. There was the exact spot I had stood! The exact spot I had felt I had been before. We had been walking down the middle of the road, and that's the spot the photo had been taken from, too. The parade ground to the left down a small hill and the barracks on the right in a neat line. Even the snow on the ground was the same. At some point while growing up I saw Dad's military pictures stored in that cigar box. While I had long forgotten them, the image was tucked way deep in my brain that sparked when I walked down that same road many years later.

✧✧✧

Prior to his illness, Dad was getting forgetful. In 2011 I received an Easter card from him, unsigned. I never mentioned it to Dad. Months later something similar came up, which prompted me to tell him. He looked at me with a beaten-up, almost shamed, look and said "I've been doing that lots lately." He was aware he was failing in certain ways, and was obviously not happy with the growing old process.

Dad and I had an arrangement. Actually, I try this with everyone. For over twenty years, work required me to travel alone for up to six months a year. That meant I picked where to eat many, many thousands of times. On any average day it was more a chore than anything else. Luckily for me in all those years, the times I had to resort to a gas station hot dog could be counted on only one hand. But it made me hate to pick, so when going out to dinner I usually request "you pick."

One evening Dad set up the route for that evening's errands, and we ended up on our way to an old-time restaurant far out in the country. Dad always liked to go out in one direction and come back in another. On this trip, we approached from the east and would leave to the west. I had not been to this spot in many years, and could not have found it without a quick look at Google maps to jog my memory of its exact location. After a nice country meal and awesome onion rings, Dad hobbled out to the car with my help, as was now the norm. He pointed me in the direction we were going to take home, and off we went.

Dad had over dinner commented about how forgetful he was getting. As we drove the rural roads Dad pointed out landmarks: There is the house where they film part of *A League of Their Own*. There is this, there is that. He would announce where I would turn long before necessary. He directed my driving for about half an hour, turn by turn and country mile by country mile. We arrived at the front door of Solarbron, the senior living community where he lived, without a single wrong turn. After putting the truck in park, I looked at him and announced, "Forgetful hell, you're like a GPS unit!"

✧✧✧

After Dad gave up his car I found myself traveling many routes and many roads I had seldom driven before. When possible Dad would "suggest" what streets to drive. They were not routes I would have logically chosen, and would certainly not find using Google Maps. He had lost his mobility, and I was his taxi. Although he never said this, you could tell his purpose was to see the whole city and not just get from place to place.

Dad and I went on a drive one sunny afternoon when I had gone out to see him earlier than usual. We drove west toward Mt. Vernon, a small town on a bend of the Ohio River less than thirty minutes away. Dad pointed out the same things he always pointed out, like "the guy who works at Solarbron lives there."

We passed the grain storage bins painted to look like kitchen canisters with huge letters: "sugar," "flour," "coffee," and "tea." We passed two BBQ joints we frequented. There was nothing we wanted to see in Mt. Vernon, so we took the bypass and headed fifteen miles north to New Harmony, another small town that sits on the Wabash River, on the Indiana/Illinois border.

In 1825, New Harmony was founded by a utopian religious community. The community failed, but there are plenty of historic buildings and sites to see. We went down the main historic strip and saw all the well-known tourist sites: the roofless church, the Red Geranium Restaurant, the peony patch, and the Labyrinth. We drove past the architecturally out-of-place Atheneum, in our view an eyesore that should just have been called the Visitor's Center. We drove under the aging-but-cool toll bridge that spans the Wabash River to Illinois. Dad and the bridge were both about the same age. It turns out they were both ending their lives at about the same time. The bridge was closed due to "structural deficiency" in 2012.

But that day we sat near the river in the truck for a little while just watching the water flow by. It was quiet and peaceful.

Heading north again we eventually connected with Interstate 64. Dad pointed out the directions, and I obliged. Nothing was said, but I got the feeling he was especially attentive to the surroundings, knowing this would be the last time he saw any of these places. I remember thinking when driving on the stretch north of New Harmony that Dad would never be here again. It made me appreciate the endless cornfields more.

We made a quick bathroom stop, where I helped Dad inside. Soon we were connecting with the often-driven Highway 41, which had changed drastically over Dad's lifetime. We stopped for pizza at Roca Bar North, a new location in a growing area north of Evansville, right on the highway. The original Roca Bar is still in its original location near the bridge to Kentucky, in what used to be an ideal place on the busy old-time highway through town. It has managed to hang on, while even the McDonalds left long ago. It still has a good following, and is usually packed in the evenings, but the surrounding neighborhood is rough, not the place you stay around outside at night. Now, families go to the new location where the large patio is filled with people and there is live music on summer evenings.

After dinner, I drove Dad back to Solarbron where he got ready for bed. We had spent the afternoon doing nothing but putting miles on the truck. We stopped only for a bathroom break and a dinner, both involving short walks on level surfaces. No steps. Nothing else. Dad was just along for the ride. He had not a care or responsibility. Cancer was catching up with him. He was physically exhausted.

✧✧✧

When I was five, Dad moved the family from Georgia back to Evansville. We had a nice house on Gum Street. We had lots of leaves in the fall, and Dad had a huge compost pile behind a large spirea shrub in the back yard. I don't know if that compost pile was planned, or lazy, but its layout made raking leaves a bit easier in the back yard. Back in those days we burned the leaves from the front yard in the gutter. We burned a stump out of the back yard once. People burned their trash. That was before the days of the Indian standing along the road with a tear in his eye.

Dad had a garden. It was mainly a rose garden. It was his thing, and he was good at it. Those were the days of the rose: The hybrid tea rose reigned before the shrub rose became popular. There were hundreds of varieties, many of which you can't find now. But they were hard to grow. They took a lot of time and a lot of care.

Dad thought I was a better gardener than he. Maybe, maybe not. I would not grow roses. I don't have the patience. But I can take a random group of plants and make a garden. My youngest son, Jared, is amazed at how I can take some of this and some of that and make it all blend together and look good.

In my garden was a little of this, and a little of that, but every day in the growing season there was something in bloom. Sometimes a little, sometimes a lot, but always something. Dad liked to stop by my house unannounced and pick flowers. He took what he could use, but always left me plenty still in bloom. I used to stop what I was doing and try to spend a few moments with him. Sometimes he cut flowers for the cemetery. When Dad could no longer cut the flowers himself, he asked me to bring him some. Because many plants bloom only once a season, I was quite aware what I was taking him could be the last ones he would see. They would be the last for his home for sure. I tried to pick the best for him. In his apartment, he always had at least one arrangement I put together for him. With lots of different size vases we usually managed to have three to five arrangements sitting around. Once, when the traditional selections in the garden were slim, I made him a rather wild arrangement I knew would be pushing Dad's limits of taste.

"We are going to put it right here in the middle of the room, and everyone will comment how much they like it," I told him.

He was very unsure. But he was also quick to tell me I was correct the next time I saw him.

On a corner nearby my home a row of yellow Tritoma was in full bloom. It was beautiful. I could not cut them because they were not mine, but I thought I could take a photo to show Dad. It would take fifteen seconds. I pushed on and kept driving to his apartment. The next day I thought the same thing, but also kept driving. After a few days, they were not so beautiful anymore. Then they stood there, past their useful life, reminding me daily how because I did not stop, Dad would never be able to enjoy their beauty.

Two seasons have since passed. I think about this every time I see them. I screwed up. I missed an opportunity. It bothers me. I let a last get by.

✧✧✧

Dad was not eating well and had zero appetite. It was easily apparent he was losing a large amount of weight. His face became sallow.

I needed to punch more holes in his belts. That was a riot as I could not find the leather punch I knew I had somewhere in my home. I did my best with an awl and hammer. I added several holes to a couple belts, and Dad was satisfied. Eventually I ran across that leather punch. Now I could add more holes and better ones than those I previously made.

At some point I was finally able to convince Dad he *needed* new pants. His were oh *so* baggy! I suggested we visit the nearby Kohl's but he would have no part of that. He was still driving, so we met at Paul's, a small local men's store located on what, in its day, was a busy west side business street—the mall of its day.

It is located a few blocks away from where Uncle George once had his feed store where Dad would go after school, and later where he worked. Uncle George's daughter, Margaret, carried on after his death. The business moved several times over the years, but always on the same street in the same general area. She passed when I was in my early teens. I still have Uncle George's oak roll top desk and some of the desk accessories and advertising pieces from the feed store. I once found a pristine advertising piece from the feed store in an antique shop in Traverse City, Michigan. It now is back in Evansville and part of the family history of the desk.

At the store, Dad was a good sport, and we got him all set up with several pairs of pants. I even had him try on several hats, and snapped photos to send to my sister, Beth, in Denver. Everyone got a kick out of his new look, but he was not a hat person.

✦✦✦

As you may have noticed, a lot of our time together centered around food. That was odd to me as it was not our norm growing up. I know in some cultures lives center around food, but that was not how I saw our family. Maybe food was a distraction to Dad and I getting together, or maybe it was our excuse to get together. Maybe this allowed his illness to take a back seat. The illness was *a* reason we got together, but not *the* reason we got together. We got together to have a nice meal, run errands, and maybe watch a ballgame. The illness became secondary.

Dad put some thought into food, or at least when he had an urge for something he was sure to try and get it. I'm sure in the back of his mind he knew it might be the last time he ever had that item. The length of his illness allowed him to say many goodbyes and have many last meals, bittersweet as it may have been. I found myself having fun with Dad's food urges. Lots of corn on the cob, and watermelon. And lots of ice cream.

One night we picked up an unused walker from Cousin Harold's house. It sat for a while in Dad's apartment until it was needed and Dad got it out. It was strange seeing Dad use a walker. I cut tennis balls to put on the bottom so he looked like all the other folks at the home. I told him he owed my dog, Kain, two tennis balls because I used a tube of new balls that had been purchased for Kain.

Later, when Dad was in a wheelchair, I rearranged the apartment to make it easier to get around. Still, the wheelchair made the bathroom difficult to navigate.

I have a photo of us going out on a nightly run. Dad has his cane, walker, and wheelchair. Prepared as a Boy Scout! Whatever we were doing that day I remember thinking it made sense to take all three.

Dad would use his walker to head to the dining area or get the mail. Once he got used to using it, I had to tell him to slow down. He was zooming up and down the halls like an Indy car racer! He was at his "new" mobile best with the walker. It was solid, not too bulky, and his strength was such he could still get around reasonably well.

Every night he had a routine of putting his *stick* up on the dresser. He would pull out a drawer and set the cane on the drawer. I just kept imaging him falling into that drawer corner and busting open his head. I finally convinced him to just lay the cane on top of the dresser. It wasn't any safer for him, but I felt better.

✦✦✦

Dad had given up driving, and I'd moved his car over to my house, but I began feeling funny having it in my driveway day after day without being driven. One day I decided to pick him up for dinner in his Mercury Grand Marquis, rather than my Ford Explorer SUV. He was surprised. He could hop right in the passenger seat. No help needed from anyone. A win for Dad. His familiar, comfortable vehicle was easier for him to get into, too—we thought. Until it was time to get out of the car. That was very difficult for him. It sat low, and with his body so weak, he could not get out without help.

I thought it would make him happy to ride in his car. I had seen him struggle climbing up into my truck. Turns out it was much easier for him to pull himself up and slide out of my truck than to slide in and then lift himself out of his car.

One evening I really crossed a line. He never said anything to me directly, but I know I crossed it. Dad was halfway in the truck struggling to lift his right leg in with his right hand under his upper leg. I was standing there to help with the door, so I put my hand out to assist. He made it clear he could do it himself. And he did. Not without effort, but he did.

From that day on I knew it was better for him to struggle than for me to take away a bit of his self-respect. Cancer was doing a fine job of taking things away from him, and I did not need to hurry it along, even if it meant Dad had to work a little harder. Every day, every battle that Dad won, cancer lost. It was better that way.

✧✧✧

Beth brought to my attention that when Dad stopped driving he started watching Mass for shut-ins on TV. A few weeks must have passed that he had not been to Sunday Mass before I found out. I'm not a regular Sunday church person. I offered to take Dad to church on Sunday mornings. He was reluctant, but he did take me up on the offer. Eight a.m. Sunday Mass was one more thing we came to regularly do together. I'm not always such a morning person either. I like to ease into the day.

Dad's church was a 100-plus-year-old beauty built for a German congregation. Not far away was the Irish church. I suppose they could follow the same religion and both pray to the same God, but not under the same roof! I find that pretty funny. I came to enjoy the old church, although Dad liked sitting right up front and I would have preferred the rear of the church so I could see more of it. It is a beautiful place with lots of details to enjoy.

There were people Dad said hello to every week and who inquired about his condition. One day after Mass there was a Sunday dinner offered in the old gym. It was early for lunch, but it was now or never. Dad was finally able to get a proper slice of strawberry pie after that disastrous slice he had weeks before at the local BBQ place. That alone made it worth the trip.

As we sat in the old gym Dad started talking. He had attended this school as a child. He remembered playing and watching basketball on the floor where we now had lunch. He talked about his school days. You could tell he felt at home and comfortable here. His cousin Harold attended this school, too. Harold loved the church and the parish. Harold's brother became a popular priest at the church.

There is one thing I did, well really *didn't* do, when I saw Dad every day. I did not ask him how he was doing. Somewhere along the way I realized it just was not a question I needed to ask. He was surely getting asked that question fifty dozen times a day.

I figured it was better if I just showed up and did my thing with him. Eventually, if necessary, he would bring up how he was, or I would figure it out from his actions. It was not uncaring; it was just the opposite. I wanted him to be able to be around me without being on the defensive, or have to cover up things to "protect" me or himself, or have to think about, and share with me what really might be bothering him.

If it was important, it would come up when he was ready, at his speed, and when he was comfortable. This avoided those shallow but polite "how are you?" questions we all pose passersby, casual acquaintances, customers, or whomever, and we really don't care much what their answer is.

I did care what Dad's answer was. The bottom line was every day he was dying a little bit, and we both knew it. How the fuck do you think he was?

✦✦✦

People can be funny about death. I wanted to visit the Municipal Cemetery in Punta Arenas, Chile, known for it very beautiful and ornate tombstones and mausoleums. I made a special effort to stop there on our last day in that city. I had the feeling Glen thought it strange and was uncomfortable just being around the place.

After Dad's passing, my son Clint was in town from Colorado. His girlfriend, Brandi, pointed out they needed to allow time to go and see Grandpa before leaving. I was impressed with her openness and respect.

✦✦✦

Dad was always very good about stopping by the cemetery. I remember as a small child visiting it at least several times a year. As cemeteries go, Saint Joseph Catholic Cemetery is a pretty one. It has rolling hills, old trees, lots of history, and grave markers of all shapes and sizes. We would zip around the large cemetery. From about age five, I knew where most family members were located.

Funerals were kind of the same. I was not sheltered from them. My parents showed us it was part of life. As I grew older I was surprised how many people I encountered who have never been to a funeral. I always thought it odd to be sheltered from things like this.

After Mom died, Dad and I frequently stopped by her grave. Sometimes together, sometimes alone, but we both went reasonably often. When Mom passed, they purchased one large stone containing both names and dates and, on the reverse side, both mine and my sister, Beth's, names. Mom had been gone over five years, so Dad had been by many times.

Early in 2012, we visited just like we had in the past, and everything was the same, but as the year progressed the visits became less frequent, and each visit seemed to be shorter than the previous one. I don't think I picked up on that right away. It really hit me one day when I just turned into the cemetery while driving Dad around. I don't think I said much to him about stopping, I just did it. That was the first time I noticed he was uncomfortable at the cemetery. He didn't want to be there. Suddenly, I realized that he knew he would be here—sooner rather than later. It was no longer a place he would be in the vague future; instead this future was within sight, not many unknown years away.

I felt like an ass. I had crossed some invisible line of dignity. I felt as if I had punched a dying man in the stomach. We left quickly.

✧✧✧

The 2012 World Series just ended. Boston got the most men around to home plate, and St. Louis left lots and lots of men on base. In 2006, I saw the final game of the World Series about twenty rows above third base. I'm glad I had that experience, but since I rarely pay attention to organized sports, you would wonder why I was ever there in the first place. However, I do love the atmosphere of baseball. I love the National Anthem. I love the beautiful green grass in the afternoon sun. I love the smell of the concession stand grilling onions to be put on some form of a dog.

As a sport, I enjoy hockey more. Hockey is a lot of sports rolled into one, and you get to fuck with the other players. It's just fun! With all that said, I go to the game, watch the game—some, leave the game and don't think about it much until I show up to the next game. I don't read about the players or think about strategy or trades or whatever. Hell, I can't even tell you most of the players' names. I just enjoy the game, the atmosphere, and the relaxation it brings me.

Dad and I were a lot alike in our attitude toward sports. He was an armchair sports fan. I never heard him discussing strategy, trades, or the like. Someone might mention something along those lines, he would respond and move on. He did go to several Notre Dame games a year, and purchased as many tickets as he could get his hands on. He was an alumnus. He liked getting tickets into the hands of people who otherwise would never get a chance to obtain them. He enjoyed their enjoyment. Notre Dame was a big deal to him. I could have cared less, and don't get it, but I'm in the minority and that's okay.

While I was growing up, Evansville was basketball crazy. Besides high school ball, it was University of Evansville Aces basketball. Dad had season tickets forever and dragged Mom along—bless her soul! I think she hated basketball more than I did.

Besides basketball, Evansville can be a bit Don Mattingly crazy. He is our Hometown Hero. I sat arms-length from him in high school homeroom for four years. Not that we were friends, or that he even remembers me, but of course I remember him.

He is a natural athlete. He could have played almost any sport well—and did. He chose baseball, or maybe baseball chose him.

What I remember most (besides liberating a case of beer out of his pickup truck bed while he played a high school basketball game) was that he was not a typical jock jerk. He did not have to prove anything to anyone, nor did he rub that in your face. Twenty years after high school I bumped into another classmate jock. He had also played some pro ball. He was an ass in high school and still an ass to this day. I always admired Donny for not being like that.

Dad loved watching Don, as did much of Evansville. By the time Dad was sick, Don's days playing for the Yankees were over, but his manager days at the Dodgers were still pretty new. That meant you had a choice of baseball in Evansville on TV—Donny and the Dodgers, or the ever-popular St. Louis Cardinals.

That's what Dad and I did many nights: We watched the game of his choice. If two games were on at the same time that he was interested in, the TV volume was muted while the radio was tuned to the other game and, if at all possible, Dad flipped between the two on TV. While I enjoyed those games with Dad, I can't say I have watched a single game on TV since. I've tried, but I just flip to something else. It doesn't seem the same now.

✦✦✦

A small wooden oval coffee table sat in Dad's living room. In the middle was always an arrangement of flowers from my yard. It was surrounded by the various cards of support Dad received; he made a point of showing them to me. He had me add new ones and remove old cards from the table. He had a spot for each one picked out, and directed me on their placement. Some people included photos, which he leaned against the vase for display.

One card and photo stand out in my mind. I am curious about the story behind them. The card was taken with him all the way to VNA (Visiting Nurse Association) Hospice when he moved there, and he set it on a shelf. The photo was of a young couple. Dad had a diverse world of friends. I will never be able to understand how he touched people or how they touched him. I think that is one area where I could improve on in my life.

Dad had a regular flow of visitors. Some stopped in once; others came numerous times. Most lived nearby, but four visitors came from far enough away they had to plan an overnight stay.

Another even flew in for a visit. I had to get that visit "approved" by Dad. I think there were some things that needed to be said between them. Some air that needed to be cleared. Neither mentioned the topic of the visit with me, and I had no reason to ask. I can only speculate. Clearing the air is more for those who remain than for those who leave.

✧✧✧

Looking back, I have two regrets with regard to my parents. One with Mom and one with Dad.

Mom asked to travel with me one week while I was working. She wanted to go to northern Michigan and visit the Bronner's Christmas store. It's a place Christmas lovers should see. Nearly two football fields of Christmas stuff are visited by about two million people a year! I tried to imagine traveling with my mom for a week, trying to work and keep her occupied. My vision was ugly! We never went on that trip. I should have just cut the work out and spent some time with her on a trip to Michigan. Still hard to imagine, but it would have been manageable.

I thought about this trip we did not take more than once when she was in her final days at hospice. The travel season after Mom passed put me down the road from Bronner's at the end of the day. I made myself stop in. Most of my Christmas ornaments remind me of travels, people, interests, and events in my life. I thought I might find one to remind me of Mom among the thousands here. Nothing, nothing, nothing caught my eye. Nothing spoke to me. Then among all those ornaments was one shaped like a Bronner's shopping bag stuffed with Christmas gifts—the one that reminds me of the shopping trip Mom wanted to make with me. That's the one I purchased to hang on the tree every year. The one that reminds me to think of mom. The one that reminds me of regret number one.

✧✧✧

I have a huge anxiety about the dentist. If it was not for my fraternity brother Brad being a dentist, I probably would not have any teeth left. I can speak frankly with Brad. I trust him. I'm as equally anxious when he is cleaning my teeth as I am when he is doing a root canal. Makes no sense. I can only surmise my anxiety dates back to childhood visits to the dentist. Of course, it could also be from watching scenes of Dustin Hoffman and Laurence Olivier in *Marathon Man*. Is it safe? Is it safe?

If Dad asked me once, he asked me fifty times to go to a Notre Dame football game with him. I had as much interest in going to a game as I did going to the dentist. Actually, I would have probably gone to the dentist first. Brad only lived three hours away, not six, and I would have felt less out of place in a dentist chair than among thousands of die-hard college football fans. I told a former girlfriend once that organized sports "were not my thing."

I had a dream one night about Dad and me being at Notre Dame on game day. We were walking down a campus road before the game. There were dorms spaced out nicely on either side of the road, and lots of happy people headed toward the stadium. I remember thinking in the dream "this is not so bad." I don't remember if that dream was before or after Dad got sick. I do know that is as close to a Notre Dame football game I ever got with Dad. Regret number two.

✦✦✦

Trash & Treasure

One evening during one of our outings we passed Dad's garage spot at his apartment building. I slowed and, without thinking, asked if he thought he would be driving anymore. It was simply an honest question that had popped in my mind, but to him it was a much more powerful question. Loss of freedom and mobility is a big deal. As Dad pondered the question I quickly tried to downplay it by adding, "just think about it, and if you don't think you will be maybe we should get rid of the garage and I can keep your car at my house in the drive." We headed to dinner, and that was that.

The next day Dad said he had given it some thought, and it would be a good idea to clean out the garage, move the car to my house, and save the monthly fee.

"Great," I said. "When can I start cleaning it out?"

After three days, and no action from me, Dad asked when I was going to get on it. He had made up his mind, and it was time to get into action.

Cleaning out his garage area was my first lesson in how to carefully and respectfully get rid of "stuff." His spot was small, but in addition to his vehicle, it was loaded with belongings. It had not been cleaned out after Mom's death, so some of her stuff was there, too. It turned out there were truckloads of goods to be taken care of.

While Dad napped, I sneaked some of his things from his garage to the dumpster, both of which were visible from his living room chair. I hauled the contents of his garage to my garage for sorting. After each dinner outing I loaded my truck with more boxes. This went on for days. Going through the material took parts of several weeks. There was so much that should have been tossed out years before, such as outdated paperwork. I kept hoping to find a bag of money. No luck though. Dad would have never hidden money.

✦✦✦

Shortly before Dad got sick I decided to sell some unneeded belongings on eBay. I was in no hurry to sell my home, but I could see it happening someday. Now and then I even hinted to Dad how it needed a family living in it again; it was too large for just me and my dog, Kain. The house had been his for twenty years and mine for maybe fifteen years. I encouraged the boys to take their belongings, warning them someday I was just going to get rid of everything.

eBay was a fun outlet for me. As I learned about online selling, I expanded my offerings. I had things I'd been collecting on and off since eighth grade, and this was all I had to show for it? I thought to myself, "I better step it up!"

So I did. The money I netted I spent on my hobby. eBay has quite a racket! They get you coming and going! Brilliant!

Then Dad got sick, and eBay became a great distraction. Using the phone app helped break up my time with Dad. I could search for things when he was with his doctors. Dad would see me bid on an item and often win. He would hear the sound on the phone when I got a bid out of nowhere on an item I was selling. After a while one of the first questions he would ask me every day was, "Buy or sell anything today?"

It was fun for both of us. I would tell him about what was going out of the house, or what was on its way to me. I told him of the positive feedback from people happy to get my junk—their treasures! I told him of the person who filed a claim against me because the cake pan I sold her did not work, and that I would not refund the money. How does a cake pan not work? She eventually claimed she did not receive the pan, but the delivery confirmation proved otherwise, so she got a "defective" cake pan and I got my money.

I told him about the lady who purchased, one after another, all the other cake pans I offered and was thrilled with them. I guess she could bake! There were sales, and stories, of the bowling ball, meat grinder, video games and players, old battery chargers, scrap strips of leather. You can pretty much sell anything on eBay, and Dad enjoyed the stories. Old becomes "classic" and "vintage." He got a kick out of it.

✧ ✧ ✧

While cleaning out Dad's garage I found several great things for my eBay sales, most of which I didn't tell Dad about. Mom had brand new sweatshirts with the tags still attached. eBay!

I did mention two items I sold. One was an autographed photo of Chip Hanauer, an Unlimited Hydroplane racer, who signed the photo to my mother, "To Carolyn, Chip Hanauer." I was not interested in keeping the photo and I didn't think my kids would keep it. It would just become clutter and get damaged, so I posted it on eBay thinking it would sell to someone in Washington or Oregon where hydroplanes are popular. I posted it for $20 Buy it Now, plus postage. Within 20 minutes, it sold to a guy somewhere in the Northwest.

I told Dad what I had done, why, and that now mom's photo would be part of a Hydroplane race fan's collection, and live forever being taken care of by someone who was willing to pay for it and could appreciate it. He saw my point and was comfortable with my decision.

The other sale I told him about was of some nice used slacks; I tried them on, but they did not fit me. I thought they had some good life left in them and selected seven pairs the same size. In the description, I wrote "perfect for a factory maintenance person where looks are important, but you don't want to overspend on slacks that could be torn or stained because of your work." I included a pair for every day of the week, and the listing was for like $25, plus postage. They sold on the first offering, and Dad liked my spin!

✦✦✦

Dad woke up in hospice late one night. "What are you doing?" he asked.

"Working on some stuff I bought on eBay. I'll stop if it's bothering you."

"No," he said, and went back to sleep.

Some people would have chosen to read. I had eBay to occupy my time. The distraction was a blessing; I found some great buys, sold some unneeded items, had great conversations with Dad, all while having some fun.

Dad wanted me to take all the extra stuff from his garage to a charity in a nearby town, which he supported in the past. It was not an easy place for me to zip by since it was quite out of my way. There was a charity I frequented more convenient to my home. I met the manager there many years before when she worked as a clerk at a business next door to a friend's business. I told Dad I had known Sandy for years, and she was doing a good job. He approved the change, but not without thought. "Just don't take anything to Goodwill!"

Somewhere along the way Dad and Goodwill did not see eye to eye, and that was that!

✦ ✦ ✦

Cleaning out Dad's garage was my first exposure to what was coming, and would take over a year to complete, or at least become manageable. The emotions associated with cleaning out the garage were unexpected. Some of the belongings I could use. Much just needed to be tossed. Some needed to find a new home via the thrift shop, and some needed to be saved for the family.

I took box after box after box of materials to the recycling bin in my alley. I thumbed through the paperwork because it was not always perfectly organized, and ran across something here or there I wanted to keep. I piled the thrift store materials in my garage and kept what I wanted. All the time feeling guilty. I was either tossing Dad's life away in the trash, giving his life away to a thrift store, or keeping his possessions. Meanwhile, he was still alive.

Dad would ask about my progress. I could not say "I threw half that crap away!" I didn't feel it necessary to tell him I sold some stuff on eBay, but I felt that was the best outlet for those items. I kept it low-key and said how happy Sandy was to get the material at the thrift store, and mentioned how helpful the staff was with unloading the truck.

✧✧✧

After Dad's passing, going through his items continued to be a necessary chore. Some were a breeze to decide whether to give away or toss. Sometimes I was overwhelmed by volume and lack of time and made a decision I regretted later. It's just part of the process.

Some items and boxes had to be put aside until I had the mental strength to go through them. It was particularly difficult when the items meant so much to my parents, but not to me. I knew I had no interest whatsoever in keeping them, but not keeping them seemed like slapping them in the face. Eventually, I worked through most of those items. It's sometimes a wonder how, after looking at a box for months without a clue what to do with the items, a spark would float through my head and I would find the perfect home.

In all that paperwork that found its way to the recycle bin, I ran across something of interest. An organization my father had been associated with many years before had offered what, for simplicity sake, I'll call an insurance policy. On a nightly outing, I gingerly asked Dad about the papers and if he knew if it was still in effect. He didn't remember it, and I could tell he didn't really care. I placed the papers aside and never brought it up with him again.

After his death, I checked around and found that, unbelievably, the policy was still in effect; upon Dad's death $10,000.00 was available to his heirs. That money would have been lost in the cracks of life had I not skimmed through all that paperwork. Cleaning out that garage and hoping to find a bag of cash really did materialize!

✦ ✦ ✦

My friend Jenny is a news producer. She knows all kinds of cool apps! One of those apps is 5-0 Radio. It's a police scanner application for the iPhone.

I started watching her productions, and sometimes we would text during her show. One afternoon while working, I turned on 5-0 Radio. A call went out and was acknowledged. The officer arrived on-scene soon to call in "shots fired." I texted Jenny: "Scanner NOW." It did not turn out well for the shooter.

In eighth grade we moved near a busy fire station. When I was younger, Dad would ask if I wanted to check out the fire. We went to several memorable fires. My mom used to tell Dad he was going to get in trouble and he must be breaking *some* law!

Dad and I talked about Jenny, her job, and the scanner calls. On occasion he would, out of the blue and just like an excited kid, say "let's listen to the scanner!" I could plug my phone into my radio and play it over the speakers in my truck. I interpreted for Dad whether the call were the city or state police, a sheriff unit, or EMS. I warned him of an important call coming and what many of the call numbers meant.

"Let's listen to the scanner!" Dad was 83 and still had a bit of kid in him!

✧✧✧

On one of our outings Dad needed more birdseed. We went to the old KMart, now a huge farm supply store of a regional chain. It reminds me of what WalMart may have looked like in its early years. No frills, good prices, huge selection, and a friendly sales staff. On Dad's list was what I can only describe as a galvanized mini trash can. To me it was terribly overpriced compared to what he could have purchased in plastic. He would not have it. Raccoons were his problem, and this was his solution. That trash can was never invaded by raccoons. It sat on his patio until after his death, and eventually made it to my garage to keep my birdseed safe from mice.

About a year later, as fate would have it, I got an unexpected offer, and I sold my home. I had to be out quickly. I opted to move to my small weekend getaway lake house 45 minutes from town. The mini trash can I protested about now sits on my porch. It is once again protecting birdseed from roving raccoons. Almost every time I open it, I think Dad is laughing at me a little. It's his way of giving me a little poke to remind me my way is not always the best way and I should be open to others' suggestions. That overpriced galvanized can served him well and now it is serving me well.

✦✦✦

Bob was a good friend of Dad's from Solarbron. He was a farmer who owned an island in the middle of the Ohio River; he had a barge to take his farming equipment out to the island. Dad would visit Bob's island at harvest time to watch the combine in action. Sometimes my boys would tag along.

Dad and Bob regularly went to breakfast on Saturday mornings at six a.m., and to Otters baseball games. Six a.m. was too early for me, but sometimes I sat with them at the games. I would stop to say hi if I wasn't sitting with them.

Dad and Bob had a favorite waitress, Bonnie, at Bob Evans. Bonnie, Bob, and Dad talked horses. Bob and Dad took Bonnie to the track. They got some good reserved seats in the air-conditioned section, and a buffet. Dad knew someone who said he could use their seats when they were not using them.

I did not meet Bonnie until after Dad passed away. He asked me to take him to Bob Evans once when he could no longer drive. It was after Bob had died. I think he wanted to say goodbye to Bonnie, but she was on vacation. I saw Bonnie sent at least one card to Dad. It had a nice note and included a photo of her and her cat. Bonnie was out of town when Dad died. I don't recall how she found out about his passing, but she cut her out-of-town outing short and came back for his funeral. She came to the funeral home, the church service, and the lunch afterwards. She was visibly upset. Someone said she had been very upset when Bob passed away, too. I guess they had their little group. It was gone.

When going through Dad's belongings there were some items I put aside for her. She just popped in my head, so they went into a box for her. There was nothing of real value to speak of, just horse racing items Dad had accumulated over the years. I went by her home to deliver them, but she was not there. I went by Bob Evans, but she was off for a few days so I left the box with the manager on duty. I never heard anything from her. I don't know if she got the box or not. If someone took it thinking there was something valuable in it boy, were they disappointed! The only things in that box were memories.

✦✦✦

While Bob was maybe ten years older than Dad, his death was unexpected. It shook Dad. He lost a good friend.

I attended Bob's funeral. Dad didn't have to ask me. I liked Bob, too. Dad thanked me for attending, and I got the feeling I relieved some burden from him by my wanting to go. I don't know if it was just companionship, or relieving him of the burden of having to request my time to attend a funeral and drive him around. Either way he seemed grateful.

Another day Dad said he "needed" to go to the funeral home to see a classmate who had passed away. Trying to be sympathetic, but also looking out for Dad's emotional state, I told him he did not "need" to do anything unless he "wanted" to.

I don't know which category attending this funeral fell into—need or want—but we did attend the showing. Dad was not able to walk far, so I wheeled him into the funeral home. I was surprised, but not many people attended. For whatever reason, I expected it to be more crowded. There were a couple of small groups gathered about the room talking as I wheeled Dad up to sign the visitors' registry.

I can't recall how the conversation started, or who it was with, but Dad was talking to a family member. It was discovered Dad had attended grade school, high school, and some college with the deceased. I didn't get the impression they were beer-drinking, go-fishing, watch-each-other's-kids-grow-up buddies, but they had history.

Dad started to tell the family about their dad and grandfather. They listened attentively. They laughed. Slowly the group grew. Eventually, almost everyone in that room was gathered around Dad listening to him speak. I patiently stood behind Dad's wheelchair. We had not entered more than ten feet into the large room. Dad managed to draw a very happy crowd. When it came time for me to push Dad up to the casket I was thanked for bringing him, the "look you in the eye, take a pause, say thank you" kind of thank you.

Years ago, I met a man at a banquet. I had been seated next to him randomly. It has been so long I have no idea what I was doing there, or why, or even who he was. I remember the typical ten-person round table surrounded by strangers, and he was seated next to me. We chitchatted. I hate chitchat. I loathe chitchat.

At a point in the conversation I looked at him and said "You knew Rudy?" Rudolph was Mom's dad who ran a little candy store. He died before I was born. I only knew him from photos. This man had known Rudy. We chitchatted a little longer, which was now even more painful to me. I finally stopped the conversation and told him I knew almost no one who had known my grandfather. I did not want to chitchat. I asked him instead to tell me about my grandfather.

I don't remember what he told me. I do remember it was nice just to meet someone who knew my grandfather, and could speak of him on a very personal level. In my life that was rare. I was grateful to have sat next to him. Maybe I don't remember anything because there was nothing earth-shattering to remember. Maybe my grandfather was just a guy with a candy store raising a family. I don't know if those people will remember the stories Dad told them. I don't. I do wonder if thirty years from now one of the grandkids might remember some old guy who knew their grandfather when he was a kid who showed up at his funeral to tell stories as the family gathered. Maybe that is enough.

✧✧✧

Just Say Yes

One day, Dad had a list of places to go and things to do. When we headed out, he directed me where to drive. He wanted to see Marsha, whom he knew from his many years of being an expert witness in Federal Court for Social Security Disability hearings. There were a number of ladies in the court office he had become friends with, and she was one of them. When I found out she didn't know we were coming I protested. We could not just arrive unannounced. But those protests fell on deaf ears.

We followed a winding west side country county road and pulled in the drive. I was told to go knock on the door through the garage.

"So now he wants me to walk through her open garage," I thought, "and knock on a door and say 'You don't know me, but my dad's in the car. Will you come talk to him?'"

Luckily for me, at that moment she needed to get the garbage cans from the street side collection point, so I was saved from leaving the security of my truck. She walked over to the truck ever so happy to see Dad. Very surprised to see Dad. She knew of his illness. As I watched them talk I could see she was very happy Dad had stopped by, even as a surprise. The visit had touched her. She was holding back tears. I felt pretty small for worrying our unannounced stop might be an inconvenience for her. I was feeling smaller thinking my protests could have prevented this brief reunion. Once again, I was touched by Dad's gesture. I was realizing I didn't understand his relationships with those in his world. Maybe it was just time for me to shut the hell up and say yes.

✦✦✦

Buzzy was Dad's longtime friend. They met many years earlier while teaching at a military school. The school had two campuses. Summers in Kentucky. Winters in Florida. On occasion, Buzzy would tell a story of taking Dad to dinner at his home. Under no circumstances, Dad was told, was he to discuss religion. If Buzzy's dad found out he was Catholic he would have been thrown out of the house.

Growing up, we visited Buzzy and his family in Georgia and Florida often. Buzzy's wife is Marie, a petite southern lady who must have had a hidden wild side to have hung out with Buzzy so long. Her brother was a kicker for Auburn back in the early 1970s. I use to crash in his room among his football memorabilia when visiting.

Buzzy is quite a storyteller. He may embellish some. He may not. I have no way of knowing for sure. If he does, it makes for a great story. If he does not, it makes for an even better story.

I have tried to explain Buzzy to my friends. I just tell them I think he is ex-CIA. That's the only way I can explain him. He is an adventurer. A teacher. Fluent in Spanish. Spent time in South America. Worked in prisons. He likes the horses. He visits lots of tracks. He knows about bullfighting. He has a handlebar moustache. He wears a kilt. He tells a story about a mobster and a corporation in South America. Picture the Dos Equis man meets Sean Connery's James Bond.

He blamed things on me like smoking. I blamed things on him like drinking. Marie and Dad knew better! He enjoys a good meal even if it doesn't meet his doctor's suggestions. Pass the salt. He sent Dad letters addressed to "The Retirement Home." I can't see Buzzy lasting long in a retirement home. It would kill his spirit. Or he would shake it up so bad they would kick him out!

✧ ✧ ✧

There are people who want to visit when you are ill. Some are fair-weather friends. Some are people who should see you only early in your sickness. There are few you really want to see before you die. There are some you should see to clear things up.

Buzzy and Marie are people who were welcome to the end. We had a great visit before Dad got too sick. He was slow, and I had warned them to break up the day with a rest period, not to plan too many activities, play it by ear. You can be frank with good friends. They respect the situation. They give, not take. Their presence brings peace and joy to a bad reality. We went to the track, ate some good meals at German and Irish restaurants, drank a few beers, and Buzzy told stories.

At the very end, there were discussions about another visit. Dad said no. I said come anyway. I knew in my heart it would be good for Dad. I also knew it would be hard on his friends. When I told them to come, I thought it would be good for everyone. In less than 24 hours Dad's condition had worsened so much the trip would have been a waste. It would have been very difficult for his friends. There was no reason to put them through such a visit. Better to remember Dad from the fun times we had earlier in the year. I asked Beth to tell them not to make the trip.

✦✦✦

Dad had lists of things for us to do. Some of the things on those lists made me uncomfortable, such as stopping by unannounced at people's homes, or asking people who were strangers to me to do a favor for Dad that he suddenly felt needed to be done. It seemed every week there were things Dad did that made me uncomfortable. As I observed the outcome of Dad's interactions my walls began to come down. Dad had a way with people—those he knew well, and those he'd just met.

Time after time I realized no one was upset except me. It was my problem, and I needed to get over it. One day I just decided whatever Dad asked for I would say "yes." Period. No discussions, no wrangling, no suggestions, no thoughts of a better way, no delay, no nothing. Just say yes.

I found saying yes to Dad concerning people issues was easy. Because I had been proven wrong so many times, I surrendered to the fact his way was right for him, and this was his life and about him... not about me.

What I had a harder time saying "yes" to concerned food. I can be very open to new foods, but generally only when traveling to new and exotic locations. I've eaten piranha, cuy (guinea pig), drunk water from a cut vine, eaten seeds and fruits hanging off trees in the Amazon, and fish I couldn't name, and will never see or eat again. All were enjoyable. But when home, I'm a boring eater. As Dad became weaker he ate less, yet he hated to waste food.

My suggestion to order what he wanted, eat what he could, and not be concerned about the waste (it was not his fault; we did ask for very small portions) did not pass muster. It was time for us to split a meal. I asked him to select the entree and side item, and I would add a side item or salad so I would be full. This worked out pretty well, except for the very few times Dad crossed my "line." One day he wanted to order a tuna salad sandwich. That was just not going to fly with me. I would have just skipped lunch! I just had to be honest and say I would not eat it, and we would both have to get our own meal. That was one of the few times I just said "no."

By chance five days before Dad would end up in VNA Hospice we were to eat dinner with Gregg and his parents. This turned out to be Dad's last dinner outing. Gregg and I talked often when Dad was sick. Prior to dinner I told him how much I was looking forward to ordering the grilled pork chops that night. I loved those chops and got them almost every time I ate at Biaggi's, a casual Italian restaurant. When the night arrived we sat at my son Josh's table (he was our waiter, and one of the reasons we chose to eat there that night). Eventually, it came time to order dinner. Around the table the orders were taken, and when Josh asked Dad what he would have Dad looked at me and said "let's split the shrimp and sausage rustica." Honestly after reading the description, this did not sound at all appetizing to me. When Dad said this, I looked across the table at Gregg, and he gave me a knowing look. I looked back at Dad and Josh, and said "OK" to splitting the meal Dad wanted, then ordered a side salad. Since that evening, about fifty percent of the time I go there I order the shrimp and sausage rustica. The first time I had it, it was a special. It is not on their regular menu. I usually have to describe it to the wait staff; what it is and how to make it. It's not difficult to order, but it usually requires a bit of discussion. That night saying "yes" led to something I enjoy and look forward to!

Beth flew in from Denver to spend time with Dad. She was staying with Dad at his apartment. He was still in pretty good shape, able to get around without too much extra help, but he tired easily. By this time, Dad and I had established kind of a routine. I was saying yes to what he asked. For a time, anyway, I was realizing the world did not revolve around me, and I was learning to go with the flow.

Beth, on the other hand, had zipped into town for a short stay. She was asking all the same questions Dad and I had already asked the doctors. She is an organizer and people person. Dad would ask me to call someone and let them know what was going on with him. This would be at 9 p.m., after spending hours with him. I was not really up to it.

Soon after he got sick I told him those kind of things were good jobs for Beth. They were talking every day anyway, so he would just add a note to his list and give her the job. That was a big weight off my back. I talked about Dad's sickness enough, and didn't want to hash it out again with someone I didn't know. Beth was isolated from the daily repetitive discussions, so going through it once on the phone with someone probably was not such a big deal. They talked in the mornings, I showed up in the afternoons. It was a good routine.

Chemo day arrived, and Beth, being a planner, had all the details. First chemo. Then Dad would go back to the apartment and rest. Then we would eat at Solarbron or a restaurant.

Beth was here for about a week. For her, it was a working visit; she would be handling her office work on the phone and computer.

Off to chemo we went. The doctor got the third degree and repeated everything we had already told Beth. As we were leaving chemo, Dad announced he wanted to go to my home and sit in the living room and eat lunch at my house.

You would have thought the freaking world stopped spinning. Beth was shocked, alarmed, and upset.

"That's not what you said we were going to do!" she told Dad.

Hello, Beth, welcome to my world!

I told her she could work from my house, but she did not

have her computer with her. We had met at the hospital, and had two vehicles with us. I just told Dad to ride home with me, and Beth could meet us later. Dad and I went home. Beth went back to Dad's apartment. I got Dad settled in the living room and poured him half a Coke. Always half a Coke. I pulled some fish out of the freezer to grill for lunch. Kain settled on the floor next to Dad's recliner. They both were happy sleeping in the middle of the day.

It was a beautiful day. The temperature was perfect. The sun was shining. The flowers were blooming. The world was clear to me that day. I was frustrated, mad, and bewildered Beth did not see it. It was right there in front of her. How could she miss it?

I walked outside and called her on the phone. I asked her to come over. Now. "This is the day you GET to spend with Dad."

It was a perfect day. Dad was here. The world was good. Next year we will not be able to spend a day with Dad. It was just so clear to me. There was nothing else more important in the world. Nothing. Today was a day we GET to spend with Dad. That was what was important.

I still think she missed out on a great day. Sure, she made it over to the house later in the day. But she missed out. Maybe it was just my moment to spend with Dad. It was an important moment. I could see it and wanted to bring her along. It was not meant to be. It was a good day to spend with Dad and do nothing. A year later that day came and went without him.

I can't say what was going on inside her. I don't know what she had on her plate. What I do know is I was told "you don't get to tell me how to feel." Yep, she was right, I didn't.

✦✦✦

The Beginning of the End

It was summer, which means fresh corn on the cob and watermelon were always available. Two of my favorite foods and often two of Dad's requests.

Sometimes I would purchase a pineapple or watermelon and take him half of it, but often even half proved too much for him. He was happy with bites.

One day at lunch, long into his illness, we were having some nice, sweet watermelon slices. They were perfect in my mind. I noticed Dad with a salt shaker in hand layering salt on a slice of watermelon. Dad had never used much salt, now I noticed he continued to sprinkle for a long time.

I started to ask what the heck he was doing putting all that salt on his watermelon. Then it hit me: His illness and subsequent treatments had removed his ability to taste. This had been coming on so slowly I had not really noticed before.

I never discussed it with Dad. There was no need to make him uncomfortable wondering if I was watching him while he ate. I figured the salt was not going to kill him, no matter how much he ate. And frankly, so what if it did? I still had the real fear of Dad lingering for months in severe pain. In the back of my mind I reasoned Dad dropping dead from some other issue could be a blessing.

✧✧✧

I never gave much thought to my home and its steps before Dad got sick. I ran up and down them all day long, and while sometimes frustrating, I figured I was getting some exercise. Since my thirties, I purposefully choose steps over elevators whenever possible and practical. Over the years, I travelled a lot for work, which adds up to lots and lots of hotel stairwells.

At Solarbron there are practically no steps. The curbs are sloped. The facility was built for people with mobility issues in mind. Until Dad had mobility problems, I was unaware of all of the steps in my house. The back of my house had one step up to the back door, so that is physically two steps into the house. When it became necessary for me to assist Dad into the house, it was a casual thing. Hold the door and stand near with an arm behind him just in case.

One day Dad's ability to climb even one step without help disappeared for good. We had a necessary discussion and review. I had to remind him he could not step with one foot onto the step, then try and take the other foot and step into the house. He no longer had the strength or the coordination. Entering my house required thought and help.

I opened the door and held it with my body. I held Dad's arm. One foot, then the other. One foot, then the other. Slow and steady. He then stopped at the bathroom inside the back door, then to the living room. I suddenly understood why lots of older people live in ranch homes.

I know people around my age who are thinking about their later years and building homes with everything they need on the main floor. No need to go to the basement or second floor. What I don't think they realize is the two steps from the garage into the home, the step up to the front porch, the three steps to the back door from the driveway may someday become as difficult to climb as Mt. Everest is for them now.

✦✦✦

Beth talked to Dad about his birthday. She had told me he did not want a party. It was easy to recognize Dad's declining health, and I'm sure he had conversations and more conversations with the many people he encountered about his condition. While I know it seems like old people only talk about their medical conditions, I cannot imagine that would be the number one thing they would prefer to speak of. It must become a chore. They put on a fake smile and say they are doing well. Or carry on for much longer than the only-being-polite asker wished to hear.

Not having a birthday party for Dad took a lot of pressure off me. I'm not much of a party planner. I could only envision all the people who would have to be invited to Dad's last birthday party.

He had had a large 80th party that was attended to room-bulging capacity. Beth planned it, and did a fine job. Family and friends came from near and far. His party was at the Log Inn. Built in 1825 as a stagecoach stop, it is a popular old-time chicken place out in the country that Abraham Lincoln visited in 1844. My grandfather also had his 80th birthday party there. If I make it that long, and if the Log Inn makes it that long, I, too, shall have my 80th birthday party at the same place.

As his birthday approached not having a party just did not seem right. Having to select a small group of his friends seemed unreasonable. While this may sound strange, we did have a birthday party for Dad. I invited none of "his" friends. There would be no probing questions. No tearful goodbyes. No stress for Dad. Instead, I planned a get-together with my friends. They all knew what was going on, so no one asked Dad any medical questions.

There were no explanations needed from me. They knew what to expect. They had all known Dad for years. Everyone had all hung out doing the exact same thing many times before. I only asked them to take turns spending time with Dad. I just wanted to make sure someone was paying attention to him while I was busy preparing food.

I purchased some pretty orange and yellow cut mums, and happened to find a plant I had never seen before at the grocery.

Being a lifelong plant person, I don't see many new plants anymore, so I bought one for Dad: a pink, potted Italian Heather *(Erica ventricosa)*. Oddly, when getting back to Dad's home, the exact same plant was on the artsy May calendar my sister always sent him as a Christmas gift. I placed one in front of the other and took a photo. You could not tell where the plant ended and the calendar began!

My friend Lisa, a teacher, did her teacher thing and made a large, artsy, and colorful Happy Birthday sign for Dad. Kim, another college friend, brought an ice cream cake with "Happy Birthday Dad" on it. As my birthday is the day before Dad's, I did get a sidebar mention on both. Lisa's poster had a small "and Chris" off to the side of the huge "Happy Birthday Frank!"

Side dishes appeared, as did some beer. There was plenty of food, and two of my son Jared's friends, Bridget and Lauren, called before we ate, so I invited them over, too. They were about one beer too many into the day, and Bridget turned out to be a riot at dinner. She was beside herself with the fresh corn on the cob and went on and on about how good it was. She was only encouraged by Gregg, who when things died down, would egg Bridget on for another show resulting in a tableful of laughter.

My friend Gregg took Dad home that evening as I still had a house full of guests. I had told Gregg no matter what Dad told him, he needed to walk him all the way into his apartment. It was getting difficult for Dad to juggle keys, a cane, pull open the outside facility door, and the like. He was just too weak to do it all safely. Not wanting to be a burden, Dad would have told Gregg to drop him off at the curb.

Later Gregg told me something I had not considered: Dad had been worried about me. He was glad to see I had a supportive group of friends. Now, he knew I would be fine after he was gone. Turns out while I was worried about giving Dad a stress-free birthday, it was more stress-free because he could take worrying about me off his list.

✦✦✦

As Dad's condition worsened, he started crossing restaurants off our preferred list. He never said as much directly, but it was happening. It had nothing to do with the food. The reason was wheelchair access and, particularly, bathroom access. Simply put, the smaller and more restricted the bathroom, the sooner we stopped going to that restaurant. It just was not worth his effort.

It is a gift to realize the importance of a moment while it is happening. A gift. I got such a gift in a men's bathroom of all places. We were with friends at Biaggi's when Dad asked to use the restroom. He was in his wheelchair, and this was a newer restaurant with nice sized aisles and easy access. The bathroom may technically have been handicap accessible, but frankly it is tight, narrow, and generally difficult to navigate with a wheelchair.

As I leaned against the wall waiting for Dad, I thought to myself "this is a bitch." An instant later I was reminded that someday, sooner than later, I would long for the chance to spend time with Dad, and take him to a difficult-to-navigate bathroom. I was instantly in a better spot. Little did I know this would be the last time we ate out, and the last restaurant bathroom I would accompany him to. Or that my small change in attitude would guide me through the tougher days soon to come.

That summer was brutal, with temperatures over 100 degrees every day. Humidity in the Midwest can be brutal, and that summer was a killer. Because of that, the last few days he was at home I brought carryout to Dad. We sat at his kitchen table and had dinner and watched baseball. Around 8:30 p.m. I headed home, which was a little earlier than usual.

Sometimes Dad would have me stick around while he showered and got ready for bed. He liked having me around just in case something happened. His process became very prolonged. It would take 45 minutes for a shower and putting on his night clothes. I would sit and watch TV and put in my time. When I left, I said goodbye just as I did every night.

That night was no different from the goodnights of the past weeks. I'd be back tomorrow to do the same again. I drove home. Most of these evening drives home the temps outside where still in the high 90s; 96 degrees at 9 p.m. with high humidity is the mark of a brutal Midwest summer! I tended to Kain and settled in for a few evening beers to take the edge off the day. At 11:30 p.m. security from Solarbron called and asked me to come back. Dad had taken a turn for the worse, and they wanted me there. I was confused as I had only left 3 hours earlier, and he was fine when I left. It was a Saturday night at 11:30 p.m. I had no idea what was to come.

I kept thinking, "Three hours earlier Dad was okay. He could reasonably take care of himself. He could reasonably get around. He could go to the bathroom, grab a snack or drink."

When I left I had no inkling that Sunday would not just be another day like Saturday. When I saw Dad, I was floored by the change. In three hours he had deteriorated so far. I would have said this was weeks, even months, in the future. In three hours his body had decided to check out. He was no longer able to care for himself in any way. He could not stand, get out of bed, go to the bathroom, or anything else without assistance. That was hard for my mind to wrap its arms around, so to speak. How in the world could his condition change so much in so little time?

✧ ✧ ✧

Hospice

I was over my head and very quickly knew it. By 1:30 a.m. I was on the phone with a VNA on-call nurse asking for help. She would get the ball rolling for care and be available on the phone, but I was on my own for the rest of the night.

Dad's bladder was telling him he needed to go frequently. Reality was different. I would help Dad up, which required us to improvise a routine to make the process manageable. He would get in position, I would grab his arms, we would move on a three count, and get him to a sitting position at the edge of the bed. He would rest and get his breath and "strength" back for the next move. I would position his walker, and on the count of three pull him up; his job was to steady himself and grab the walker. Now we inched to the toilet only feet away where I supported him while he went. Now back to the bed with the help of the walker and reverse the process to get him back to a sleeping position. That would wear him out, and he would sleep until the next time. We repeated this process several more times in a few hours.

Dad had a pretty sweet setup at Solarbron. They provided breakfast and lunch at two seating times, and I took him out to dinner. He had ladies clean the apartment and could get his hair cut on certain days, and even get rides to the grocery store, or doctor's office, or the like. There was little need for him to have much in the way of cleaning supplies. After his many trips to the bathroom that night I needed some. The best I could find was a terribly old pink can of Lysol spray, the bottom rim rusted away by time. I would spray parts of the bathroom with Lysol, do my best to paper towel the area clean, and wait to do it all over again in a short time.

By 3 a.m., I told Dad I was going up to the security office and ask him to please find me a hospital-style urinal that could be used in bed. I needed him to go next door to the sister facility that offers higher care levels and find one. A bit later he knocked on the door and had a shiny new box with what turned out to be an item I will never again take for granted—a $6 plastic male urinal. God, what a lifesaver!

✦✦✦

Dad and I both knew things had changed overnight and life was going to be different from here out. I told Dad I had to get help, as his care had surpassed my ability and knowledge base. There was no hesitation or fight from him. He knew he had gotten much weaker overnight and his condition had worsened.

I made lots of calls, pushed, pulled, and prodded, but nursing help or a higher-level care room were not available until Monday. It was going to be me taking care of Dad, or I would need to put him in the hospital. Those were my choices for the next 24 hours or so. At one point, a Solarbron employee stopped in, and I said I needed 45 minutes to make the round-trip home, but I would really be gone a little longer. I had to run home to let the dog out and grabbed a bag of clothes so I could shower at Dad's apartment.

When the VNA nurse finally showed up on Monday and Dad was in capable hands, I immediately left to attend to the dog, take a shower, and get a short mental break. Within about four hours he was transferred to the higher care facility next door. I opted to maintain personal VNA nurses for him instead of only having a floor nurse and staff attend to him. We both liked that setup. For the next day or two he would be properly cared for and have some new women with whom to share stories!

Later I got a call from a VNA contact. "Your dad has done a lot for VNA in his life. We would now like to return that favor. We want to care for your Dad at VNA."

Everyone was concerned that it was a little (but not a lot) early to check Dad into a hospice facility. Dad had his reservations, too. Hospice is "Hotel California," you can check in when you like, but you never leave. I can say that now with a smile on my face and the peace of knowing what a special place the VNA is.

That evening, I spoke with Dad about it before heading home and simply asked him to consider it. No pushing. No emotion or arm-twisting.

The one hesitation Dad had about going to VNA Hospice was my dog. I brought Kain out to see Dad on a regular basis, and they were fond of each other. Kain was not allowed in the apartment, but no one told on us, and Dad really didn't care, which was odd to me because he was a rule follower.

I called the VNA contact and said that being able to see the dog was the only thing holding Dad back from the move. Five minutes after ending our phone call she called back to say "higher powers" approved Kain's visits and all would be fine. No dog hassles. We could enter through the garden area, make our way to Dad's garden door and never disturb anyone. When I told Dad Kain could visit he was ready to say yes to being admitted to Hospice.

As soon as Dad turned worse, I told Beth, "You need to make plans to see Dad now!" She questioned me, saying I'd told her similar things in the past. That other "now" was so she could enjoy being with Dad before he got too sick. This "now" was a "before he is gone" now.

I was pissed and told her bluntly if she saw Dad's condition she would not question me.

✦✦✦

A local ambulance service took Dad from Solarbron to the VNA Hospice. Two young men showed up, probably in their mid-20s and looking wet behind the ears, but nice enough and overly qualified to drive a dying man to his deathbed. Dad, still flanked by a VNA nurse, a Catholic priest, Jeremy, who was a longtime family friend, and me, was loaded up and carted off to Hospice.

We all made our way there in separate vehicles, and naturally all arrived faster than the ambulance. It was only a short drive. On a bad day in horrible traffic, the drive could be made in 20 minutes. In just this short time the attendant could not say enough nice things about Dad. He had gotten the short version of Dad's life in that drive. People, places, things.

Dad was being transferred to his room, and while doing paperwork this young man went on and on about Dad's life. He repeated in detail and enthusiastically to me things Dad had done, places he had been, and so forth. He seemed as truly impressed with Dad's accomplishments as I was this young man's admiration of my father's deeds.

Here was a man on the way to his deathbed still making friends and creating a spark in someone so quickly, and in such dire times, giving and not whining about things to come, or what he wished could be.

When I was in eighth grade I had a teacher who later became a family friend. At the time he was a Deacon. Later he became a Catholic priest. He fit right into our family and tolerated (or moderated maybe) all of our dysfunctions! Jeremy was a staple at many holiday meals, or just hanging out taking a break from his world to sit in our home and watch a movie. He was able to be himself, and generally the only "official" duties he had to perform at our home was blessing the meal. My parents grew fond of him and stayed in close contact even as my contact lessened as I had a family and increasing responsibilities and distractions.

Jeremy always made himself available for me when I had difficult times in my life. Once, during a difficult time he told me he would pray for me but "really wasn't sure what to pray for." I responded, "Just pray God knows what I need."

Jeremy made it into town every so often and stayed in touch with Dad. Sometimes we would all meet for lunch or a quick visit at Solarbron. The day Dad was moved to VNA Hospice, Jeremy arrived at Solarbron early to spend time with us.

After being transported to VNA and when Dad was settled in his new room and things quieted down, Jeremy asked Dad if he would like to receive Last Rights. Last Rights is the sacrament given to Catholics shortly before death. It seemed too early to me, but it made sense as Jeremy was close with Dad, in town, and available, and who knew what was in Dad's future. Jeremy stood at Dad's left, and I was at his right. Jeremy recited the prayers.

Dad was at peace knowing he had received Last Rights. It brought him a deep comfort in his soul. Dad would have been grateful to receive Last Rights from any priest, but receiving them from Jeremy was particularly comforting.

Dad prepared his entire life to enter heaven, and this was just one more step in that direction. He truly believed with his whole heart, and the thought of heaven brought him peace. At the same time, this was one of the few times I saw him struggle with his mortality. I could see it in his eyes. Not fear. Not regret. I never saw him looking for a "do over." I don't think he ever tried to negotiate or deal his way out of his sickness.

The Last Rights imparted a certainty to Dad's future, acknowledging that it would not be a long one here on Earth. There was a sadness in that realization. A sadness of things that would end. Spending time with friends and family, reading, watching Notre Dame or Cardinals games, feeding the birds, petting a dog, talking with his grandchildren, seeing great-grandchildren that had yet to be even conceived, all those things that one holds dear.

Dad had some good days at VNA Hospice. He settled in comfortably. The surroundings and many of the employees were familiar with him, and he could get into his wheelchair and get out of his room. On one of the trips we stopped at the various recognition plaques around the halls. Dad's name was in multiple places. He had spent countless hours in support of VNA, and now they were supporting him in his final hours. We went into the public areas and spoke with other visitors.

One afternoon the television room was crowded with a family. Dad and I were in the doorway. He asked a young man to climb the bookshelves to retrieve an angel. It was the angel Dad donated after Mom's death. There were many angels that made their home here. Dad held it in his lap, and when we returned to his room he told me precisely where to place it so he could see it from his bed. I can only speculate the angel was a happy reminder he would soon see Mom again.

✦ ✦ ✦

As I mentioned, Dad had been named Harold's Personal Representative. While at the bank one day, shortly after Harold died, I asked his attorney, Tim, if Dad could watch the Fourth of July fireworks from the comfort of his office on the riverfront. Tim, of course, said sure.

It never happened. By the Fourth of July, Dad was in hospice. He could travel the halls in his wheelchair. As the fireworks launch time approached I suggested he get in the wheelchair and go out to the parking lot to watch the show. We were not far from the riverfront and would have a good view.

Evenings were still steaming hot, and Dad simply did not want to mess with it. Not wanting to give up so easily I went to the garden outside Dad's room and placed a chair next to the tall, brick wall. Stretching tall on the arm of the chair and standing on my toes, I held my iPhone over the top of the tall, garden wall recording what I could. Dad's last fireworks were viewed on an iPhone as he lay in his hospice bed. He seemed okay with that.

✦✦✦

At the VNA Hospice there is a lot of flexibility in care. People come to spend the last hours or days of their life. Usually they get what they want. My mom just wanted to be left alone when she was sleeping. Dad got to have Kain visit.

There are certain protocols and procedures that still must be followed, an umbrella under which there is some flexibility. Those are my words. The medical field probably calls them something else. In Dad's case I would go along with things until they didn't make sense. I went along with him taking care of his finances, until he could no longer take care of them in a timely manner. I went along with him driving himself until he popped a tire when he drove into a curb. I went along with no radical surgery.

I was at peace with Dad's DNR (do not resuscitate) orders much faster than I was when Mom was in hospice. I had learned much from watching her passing and from conversations about DNR orders with a nurse I dated for a while. I also had a private conversation with Dad's doctor.

I had several back and forth conversations at VNA about checking his blood sugar levels. It got to the point when he was only days from death, but still aware of what was happening around him. He was not going to die from diabetes.

"If he dies today from complications due to diabetes his death certificate is still going to say pancreatic cancer as cause of death, isn't it?" I asked a nurse.

"Yes."

"Quit pricking his finger."

Testing his sugar bothered me more than it bothered him. Dad was under such a high dose of pain medication a finger prick was unnoticeable. I guess I felt I should be looking after him. It seemed unnecessary. That's why it bothered me.

✦✦✦

Pain. That concerned me. Pancreatic cancer can be painful. Very painful.

Considering Dad did not have the highest tolerance for pain, he didn't do much complaining. Many years earlier, Dad had a bad experience with a catheter following his prostate surgery. He had more difficulty recovering from the catheter pain than all the other stuff associated with that surgery combined.

With the cancer, as Dad weakened his frequent bathroom visits became quite a chore. He was physically unable to make any bathroom visit without help. He was too weak. No matter the physical cost to himself, he tried because he just did not want a catheter.

I was afraid we would break his arm when helping him out of bed. It took some coordination between Dad and whomever was helping him. Lots of timing and lifting and shifting. It was difficult for Dad, and I did not look forward to the whole process. It was necessary, but not easy. Physically or mentally.

✦✦✦

Part of the dying process is surrendering. It starts very early in life. Funny to think the process of dying starts when you are young. You surrender your childhood to become an adult. You surrender your freedom when you have children. You surrender to your job. You surrender your strength as you age. You surrender fearlessness with responsibilities. You surrender your mobility, your memory, your steadiness, your eyesight, your hearing, your taste. You surrender your modesty.

Hospice was another series of surrenders. The first few days he functioned. We had a bathroom routine. There would be no catheter. Dad got weaker. Movements became more difficult. The nurses let us know there was another option for Dad: adult diapers. It feels weird and invasive to tell, but it is the truth. It bothers me to write this. But the reason I do is because Dad was so much happier once he surrendered to them. At that point, I don't think it was much of a surrender. Physically, he could be left undisturbed and comfortable for longer periods of time.

His mind was telling him he needed to go to the bathroom, but reality was different. He rested better. His body continued to shut down, his food intake diminished, his liquid intake was not by mouth. He no longer needed to leave the bed. He could rest.

✦✦✦

Dad had been at VNA a number of days. My being there with him as much as possible disrupted whatever unimportant routine I had been following. By the time Beth arrived, I was stressed. I worried Kain was not getting enough attention and that the lawn needed cutting. Just stupid, ordinary, life stuff that was falling through the cracks.

Beth showed up with her kids Brandt, Elly, and JJ. She was all peppy and had a plan. She wanted to, right then and there, get Dad's car from my house for her stepson to drive. She wanted to do things her way. That was not going to work for me.

My agenda for when she arrived was to get out of there and take care of me and my needs for a few hours. I just needed to unwind. When she figured out she was not getting her way, she restated what I had told her I was going to do, but made it sound like her idea.

"Isn't that what I just said?" I asked.

I left VNA with nothing in mind, but knew it would be several hours before I returned. I ended up at The Pub and had a hamburger and beer. It was a good start toward unwinding and taking care of myself for the first time in days.

Generally, Beth and I get along fine, but we are a bit different. Politically, Dad and I held the same views. Beth is somewhere the hell way out in left field. If Beth and I enter a room of strangers, I prefer to sit down with one person and have a conversation for the evening. Beth meets everyone, learns their life stories, and has their email addresses. That said, Beth had lots of friends stopping by to visit. That was fine. I like them. Her friends are good people. Hell, having a sister just a little younger was great while growing up. It led to me dating a number of her friends!

What irritated me was the noise. I could tell when Dad was not comfortable with Beth having friends in the room laughing and talking loudly. I was probably more in tune with his feelings at that time. I had watched him for months.

Sometimes it was fine. Other times it was not. I could just tell. I would encourage them to go to the family room. There was a quiet kitchen, a chapel, a garden. There were plenty of places to chat. I asked my friends to encourage them politely to leave the room. I stood outside the room to chat with my friends—hint, hint.

At one time Dad and I talked about the noise. He agreed with me that Beth didn't get it. Dad had no problem with the visitors and for the most part enjoyed them stopping by. He found it comforting himself and knowing there were people supporting his kids.

Eventually, we posted a note on the door for visitors to check in at the nurse's station. It was hard to explain to people Dad could not interact well. He was not going home. He was tired. Some folks got it. Some did not.

Before Dad passed away a retired general Dad knew stopped in to see him. Dad was unresponsive, as he had been for days. The general understood. I didn't have to explain things to him. He stayed a brief time and left. He was the last person to visit Dad. Fifteen minutes later Dad was gone.

✦✦✦

VNA is a comfortable place. Dad had been on the Board of Directors for over 20 years. I never paid much attention to the place. I heard the name, but never went by to check it out or anything. I was quite impressed the first time I went inside the hospice. Dad was on the building committee. They had done a fine job researching and working on the design. Dad's name hangs throughout the halls with others who have been involved and supported the organization over the years.

One winter day, before Dad got sick, there was a fundraising gala, which Dad asked me to attend. I felt out of place. It went well and was crowded. Because of the crowd, seating became a bit awkward. I guess that's a good problem. The following year the fundraiser was moved to a local country club. It was a much better arrangement. I sat with Dad and some well-connected volunteers and higher level employees. When my mom had been at VNA Hospice years earlier, I spent the night on a chair that converted into a bed. It was not uncomfortable. It was very convenient and allowed me to be with my mother when she died.

There was an auction during the event. You could bid on needed things, such as kitchen items, carpet for a room, televisions, hospital beds, and the like. By now the building had some age on it, and there were things that needed replacing and updating. Just general wear and tear taking its toll.

Items came and went. I asked a lady at our table if the chair would be one that folded out into a bed. The answer was yes. I told her I would buy one for the hospice. Dad gave me a very surprised look. I responded with a smile and said "you just bought half of it," but I was fully ready to pay for it all if he had objected. Later my sister offered to pay a third. It was a nice way for us to remember and give back for Mom's time at VNA.

There were several chairs to choose from in Dad's room. The first night I did not stay with Dad. He was in good care, so I could relax. I knew harder days were to come. Pacing myself was in order.

One evening I was talking with Dad and discussing going home for the evening. It was at least 9 p.m., and a Cardinals game was winding up. I could tell he did not want to be alone, so I just asked him if he wanted me to stay the night. He said yes. From that evening on someone stayed with Dad every night until he passed away.

I would often sit in a chair just past Dad's feet. When he looked straight ahead we could see each other. It was where I was sitting when he passed away. I saw Dad wake up many times, glance my way, and go back to sleep. Knowing someone was in the room with him brought him some peace. There is not much you can give a dying person. There is not much a dying person needs. Peace, love, reassurance, and your time.

✦✦✦

When you are in the hospital people bring magazines to help occupy the time. I cannot imagine what I would want to read about in my final days. What could possibly hold my interest? What could matter? I continued to bring flowers to Dad's room as I had done for him all summer. I took the extra flowers to the nurses' station. I took small breaks during the day to take care of my dog and unwind. I could clear my head for a bit at home, which, fortunately, was only a few minutes' drive away. Sometimes friends would sit with Dad for a few hours to help me out. I spent as much time as I could with Dad. That is what I had to give him that mattered. Time.

If he woke up to see me sitting in a chair, and if it was comforting to him, then it was worth my time. If I could turn the TV channel without him having to ask a nurse, or get ice cream for him, it was worth my time.

While in college and after I had a landscape business with my dad. He was the money, and I was the muscle. We had three bright green trucks, employees, a beautiful new blue Ford tractor, and all the stuff that goes along with that business. We did well and opened a retail place—the year it was 100-plus degrees from May 1st on! It was not good.

Around this point in my life I had two boys, Clint and Josh, and shortly later a third, Jared. My wife was working, too, but there never seemed to be enough to pay all the bills. It was a hard, poor time for me. Kids really eat into a budget! We needed a full-time sitter, and a friend referred us to Angie.

My wife and Angie became good friends, and the boys loved her. Angie was young and bouncing around finding her place in the world. Not in a bad way, just in a young way. I put one condition on her employment. Angie had dropped out of high school; if she were going to work for us, she had to pursue her GED. She did work for us, and she did get her GED. A win for all of us.

✧✧✧

Angie's Aunt Ruth lived at the opposite end of our block. Even after we moved to my parents' former home we were still only a few baseball-throws from Ruth's home. Angie continued to stop in to say hi to the boys, or to show off her own children, for many years.

Evansville is a place still small enough that it often seems that everyone knows each other. Ruth was also related to a close high school friend of mine, so sometimes we crossed paths at that family's reunions or funerals. And of course, my parents knew Angie fairly well, too.

It was still a surprise when Dad arrived at VNA Hospice to see Angie in the hallway. Her mom had been there for some days already. She found out my dad was on his way in. When Dad got settled, and the time was right, I told him Angie was here with her mom. It was one of those bittersweet things. You hate to hear someone is so sick, but if that's the case then you are glad they have such a fine place to spend their final days. Later Angie, her husband, Brendon, along with Aunt Ruth, came to visit with Dad.

✦✦✦

One afternoon, while in the hall, Angie approached me and said her mom had just passed. I felt for her, but we all knew her suffering was over. I had to get my mind in order and wait for a good time to tell Dad. After about twenty minutes I walked to the side of his bed and told him.

He looked at me, unmoving, for a few seconds, then raised his right arm, offering me his hand, and said "let's pray for her." He proceeded to say the "Hail Mary" aloud and alone while I held his hand. I could not utter a peep. I was stunned by his action. When he was finished, I gathered myself and apologized for leaving him to do all the praying alone. I told him I had said every word but just to myself, but if I had opened my mouth I would have cried.

I did not say how stunned I was by his actions. At 51 my dad floored me on his deathbed. Here was a man who could have chosen to be unhappy with his situation. He was days away from death himself, he had his own shit to worry about, his own pain, his own family, his own friends, his own worries. Yet, without hesitation, he gave of himself to pray for another. It was his first thought: "Let's pray for her." He wasn't trying to impress anyone. That didn't come from attending mass once a week, or doing right only when people are watching. No, that comes from a lifetime of good. A lifetime of caring about others. A lifetime of giving of yourself. A lifetime of being the man called Frank Kern.

✧✧✧

Bryan is my college fraternity brother. We called him "Wolfman." He was an expert at crashing cars. Thank goodness he is past those days! We hung out together with our wives. We each had three kids. He got divorced; so did I. The wives are gone, but we're still friends.

God put Wolfman on this earth to listen. I've told people close to him that. I've told people close to me that. If it had not been for Wolfman, I might not be here today. That sounds dramatic, but it could be true. I'm glad I won't know.

When I was going through my divorce, Wolfman spent lots of time listening to me. Way more than anyone would want, but listen he did. He didn't say much, but I remember him telling me I had to quit thinking thoughts that were eating me up inside. He was right. We drank a lot of beer while he listened. I was not in a good place, and without Wolfman, I don't know what stupid thing I might have done or what trouble I'd have gotten into. But because he sat and listened, I did not do anything too stupid. He helped me get through it, one tough day at a time. I can never repay him. There are no words to express my appreciation.

There are two things Wolfman has a talent for: listening and eating. Years passed and if I had friends over, Wolfman could be counted on—particularly if there was food. So long as he didn't have a conflict with his three daughters' schedules.

When Dad was at VNA Hospice Wolfman stopped by. Dad was in serious decline. He was medicated, groggy, weak, and his voice faint. There were several of us in the room. Wolfman approached Dad's bed. They talked for a few moments, and I could tell Dad did not remember Wolfman. Then, a light bulb went on, all the pieces fell together; Dad knew who he was. "You have three girls," he said.

Wolfman took Dad's hand and bent to listen. He stayed like this for ten or fifteen minutes. Wolfman listened to Dad's hard to understand speech. He gave Dad the only thing that mattered, attention, patience, and love. I had to leave the room twice. Wolfman was put here to listen. It's his gift.

✧ ✧ ✧

I made only a few notes during the time Dad was sick. The notes I did make were when he was in VNA Hospice. It was important to me that I did not forget. I wrote these things when Dad's time on earth was very short.

I noted it was 4:45 a.m. Tuesday. Dad had awakened.

"You taught me lots the past six months," I told him.

"I bet I have."

I wrote he said I had been a "faithful son." He told me "you've been wonderful through all this."

I often spent the night at the hospice. Dad would only become very present for a brief time overnight. He was sharp and aware. After realizing a pattern of these late night, reasonably normal (all things considered) chats, I wanted to stay with Dad so I could enjoy him as he had been. It was purely selfish on my part. These moments were significant.

I wanted this time with him. Beth decided to stay with Dad one evening. I considered trying to talk her out of it knowing any day this could come to an end, but that did not seem right. Instead, I alerted her to the fact Dad had been waking up in the middle of the night very able and willing to talk. When I arrived the next day, she was happy to announce that she was blessed with a great visit with him in the middle of the night.

Later, when speaking with a friend about these moments with my dad, I said it was a time I knew I could ask him anything I wanted. I was aware each night might well be my last chance. Many questions bounced around in my head. I have no idea which questions I pondered. I do know I told my friend any questions I could think to ask I already had had answered, having just spent the last six months with Dad. That's a big deal. Any question not already answered was woefully insignificant.

One question I asked concerned prayer. Could prayer be kept uncomplicated? He thought for a while and answered yes. He did more for my spiritual health in a few seconds than all the years he dragged me to Catholic school.

✦✦✦

I noted one amazing thing about the conversations I had with Dad. "Moments become eternity; seven minutes become like thirty."

On two separate nights I looked at the clock when Dad woke and I spoke to him. Two nights questions bounced around in my head. Two nights I know those moments were very real and cherished. And two nights, if you had asked me how long Dad was lucid I would have told you we sat there for thirty minutes together. The reality was we had seven minutes. Those were the slowest moving, longest, and best seven-minute periods of my life. Seven minutes and time stood still. Had there not been a clock, and had I not been aware to look at the clock, I would swear we talked for thirty minutes. Seven.

Tom was a friend of Dad's for as long as I can remember. Thirty years ago, I remember doing landscaping work for him at his home and the business where he was the director. Long story short, for the past twenty years I've had the feeling Tom was fighting an uphill battle not of his making. Life just kept throwing him curve balls, but Tom carried on.

At the hospice, every day Tom showed up with his Bible in hand to pray with Dad. I liked his faith. He came to the hospital, he visited Dad's apartment, and he came to VNA every day. He didn't require attention. He came, he prayed, and when he felt it was time, he left. He did not distract. He added.

✦✦✦

Tom sat by Dad's bedside reading the Bible. I sat near Dad's feet fiddling with my iPhone. Dad had not been responsive for days. Nothing in that room had changed for days.

"Well, there you go." That is what I said to break a long, speechless streak. Tom looked up at me. I was looking at Dad. Dad's labored breathing had just stopped.

I'm reminded of a scene in the movie *Forrest Gump*. Forrest says, "If I'd a known this was gonna be the last time me and Bubba was gonna talk, I'd a thought of something better to say." It just seems I could have come up with something better to say than "well, there you go."

Tom was on Dad's right, and I moved to his left. I called the nurse and then my sister. Dad passed away with five people at his side. For a man who did not want to be alone I'd say he did well.

✧✧✧

Seven months went by from diagnosis until Dad passed. Dad looked pretty normal for several of those months. He got around well. He ate well. Everything seemed pretty normal. But then the cancer started to get ahead of him. A little at a time it gained ground. Slowly at first. No change for months, then you could see change over weeks. Then hours.

The changes that took place in hours were frightening. I remember when I has a kid, Dad had a bit of a gut. He slimmed down in his later years. When the cancer really kicked in he lost lots of weight in months. It was easy to see, though I probably noticed it less than others as I saw him every day. By the time he passed away he looked like a concentration camp survivor. It was unbelievable what cancer did to his body from the inside out.

Finale

Dad had just passed away. Beth and I met with Jerry, the same funeral director who had handled Harold's funeral. A former neighbor and family friend, he'd known both my parents well. Mom had spearheaded preplanning their funerals, and the hard work was long past; there was not much to do. There were not many costs remaining for us to bear, and few details to address. Jerry asked for photos of Dad. We reviewed paperwork. As we stood in the lobby to leave, Jerry casually reviewed the few things we needed to bring him. He mentioned we did not need to bring shoes. I jokingly responded, "We should bury Dad in his Crocs!" Beth thought that was a great idea. Dad was buried in the Crocs he loved.

Clothing was not an issue. Dad had worn a sports coat his entire career. He had dozens of dress shirts and ties. Even being retired for over ten years, he still had a dozen sports coats hanging in his closet.

I met Beth at Dad's apartment where she was staying. There was no shortage of photos to choose from. Dad still had a poster collage from his 80th birthday party that Beth had designed, so we included it, too.

Beth asked me if I was planning to keep any of Dad's clothes. I said I suspected I would if I found some that fit. She selected a coat and commented something like "this must have been the one he wore last because it is right here in front." It was nice looking, and I thought I might want to keep it for myself. It had been a few years since I purchased any dress coats, and I could use a few "new" ones. I tried it on. The sleeves stopped about five inches too short! The shoulders were tight. "No way am I keeping this one!"

I was not going to keep it. Problem solved; she set it aside for Dad. We selected a shirt I had recently picked up from Dad's dry cleaner. We chose a Notre Dame-colored tie.

✧✧✧

My three boys drive me nuts sometimes. They run on their own time. I expect it from them. Sometimes it's no big deal. Sometimes it's very disrespectful. It doesn't make me happy, but I expect it. At Dad's funeral, I bent over and whispered in one of their ears, "if any of you are late for MY funeral I'll have you written out of the will."

I was at the funeral home early. My sister was running later than expected, which was not typical for her. Jerry and I were talking in the lobby when she finally showed up. She announced the reason for her tardiness was she had been looking for a suit that had been hanging in Dad's closet. It seems the nice suit we had selected belonged to a friend, and was not actually Dad's.

I've come to find out many people do not know this about dressing the deceased. I did not. When making preparations for the funeral, to ease with dressing, their clothing is cut in half down the middle of the back. There would be no fast, easy removal of the sports coat. What was done was done. Dad got the last laugh and got to wear a "new" sports coat at his funeral.

After declaring at Cousin Harry's funeral that he did not want a military funeral, he ended up with one. The funeral was a little crazy. There were two funerals in the same section of the cemetery at the same time. The other funeral parked really stupidly so we could not get to our area. We had a LONG delay on a HOT day. We waited in our cars with AC blasting until they moved off so we could park.

Meanwhile, the poor military group had been standing in the HOT sun for some time. Usually the military portion is after the religious portion of the funeral. Jerry asked if we minded him doing the military part first so those poor guys and gal did not have to stand there any longer than necessary. So that is what we did.

Over the years, I helped Dad dispose of several relatives' belongings. I helped at my grandfather William's house and have a peaceful feeling when I think back on it, but have no idea why. I helped clean out his Cousin Margaret's home and business. She kept everything, and in general she had a different outlook on life than most everyone else. She was not a conformer. We discovered she hid her few valuables in the oddest places.

Dad's rent was thousands of dollars each month, so to drag out cleaning out his apartment would have been costly. My youngest son, Jared, and my sister, Beth, flew back to Denver shortly after Dad's funeral. My middle son, Josh, was busy with work, and struggling with Dad's death. My oldest son, Clint, was able to stay in town to help.

We hit it pretty hard. Clint liked getting up early and finishing early. I liked getting a later start and working late. I won more often than not. Clint still got to see many of his friends and hang out with them after helping me all day.

We set aside boxes for various family members, which we filled with items we thought they could use. We set aside items for the thrift store. We set aside items for friends. I made piles to go to my house for later sorting. We would load the car and truck and head to the thrift store—load after load. We borrowed a large trailer and moved furniture. We gave some away, and hauled other pieces to my garage. Clint carefully wrapped fragile items and securely packed them, adding a brief description to the outside of the box.

This went on for hours a day for weeks on end. I juggled meeting with lawyers, banks, and the like, sometimes with Clint and sometimes without him. Considering the stress of it all, things went pretty smoothly.

Did I mention the heat? All this went on with miserable outside temperatures and horrible humidity. One day I made the mistake of leaving a stick of deodorant on my car seat; the entire thing melted. MELTED!

✧ ✧ ✧

There were still many of Mom's items in the house: seasonal decorations, crafts, treasured travel purchases. I was glad to find homes for most of them. Mom had helped at children's libraries since I was young. Many of the decorations found a home with my friend Lisa, a teacher. Mom would have approved.

When going through the belongings it went from easy to impossible. Unattached to attached. Businesslike to sentimental. I would make great progress, then find a box of old photos, stop for a moment to look at a few, then realize twenty minutes had passed. Had Clint not been there I would have spent many extra days or weeks going over their belongings. He gave me the necessary time to look over items, and patiently listened to my stories, but eventually moved me along. Doing the job alone would have been a nightmare.

When Dad retired from the EAB they allowed him to keep his company car, the Grand Marquis, as a retirement gift. It was an old-school car. It drove like a dream and had lots of bells and whistles. Come to find out it could hold lots, and lots, and lots of belongings. We would load it up—or try to. Its content-holding ability was like the Grand Canyon. Once, when we arrived at the thrift shop and started unloading cart after cart of material, one employee asked, "is this all for us?" It was like watching the clowns come out of a little car at the circus. The Grand Marquis just kept giving up the goods!

We had lots of boxes and small furniture items to send to Denver for Clint and Jared, my sister, and her family. Beth suggested we give the car to Clint for his time helping clean out Dad's apartment, and have him drive it home to Denver loaded with everything, saving us money on shipping.

Clint needed a vehicle, so he liked the arrangement. I had him "lose" some items to show up later that year as Christmas presents from Grandma and Grandpa. Then there was a box or two that really got lost for a while. I didn't know if he was kidding me about this or not, but they showed up under the tree in time to make a big splash with my sister.

✧ ✧ ✧

I did a final walk through the apartment. A charity was scheduled to arrive later that day to pick up the last items for donation. Maintenance would let them in. Everything was in order, but before leaving the apartment and returning the keys I left a note on the kitchen counter...

"Ladies and Gentlemen
Frank and Carolyn have left the building."

It had been maybe a month since Dad passed away when I received a call from Solarbron that FedEx had delivered a package for Dad. When I saw what it was, I knew I had to see Dad's attorney soon.

I met with Bill at his office. I had not even opened the package when I handed it to Bill. Earlier in the year Dad had contacted Bill about this specific issue and was told to just drop off the paperwork and he would handle everything. I had slipped some info under his door one day, and in moments we would see the fruits of his labor.

I sat opposite Bill at his desk as he opened the package to reveal a stack of Notre Dame football tickets. Dad had done well this year. He got all but two of the tickets he wanted for the year. Usually he did okay on the ticket lottery and got a reasonable amount of tickets. One year he got only two. This year he nailed it. The year he was gone, and he could not go to a game!

Earlier Bill had taken Dad's information and filled out all the paperwork and sent in a deposit. Dad wasn't able to do it at the time. Bill is president of the local Notre Dame booster club and coordinates an informal ticket exchange among its members. Dad had participated in this give and take for many years. Dad really liked getting tickets into the hands of people who would otherwise never be able to get them. He had one strict rule: The tickets cost you face value and you could not sell them. I met many appreciative people over the years who got tickets from my dad. He did really enjoy doing that for people.

✦✦✦

What started off as an effort to avoid the confusion and stress of spending all day Christmas Eve with my in-laws turned into a holiday tradition for me. I had a short list of friends I would spend the day stopping by unannounced at their homes dropping off a Christmas gift. Sometimes I would stay a few minutes and sometimes hours. Close friends, Chad and Angie, always had family over that day, but with their official invitation guests were put on notice that "Chris will be stopping by." They came to expect my visit.

For about thirty years this was my tradition. I enjoyed it. Last year I stopped. I didn't realize I had stopped until the day came and went. I had moved. Life had changed. I had changed. What became the last year of my tradition was a different year of deliveries. It was a long day. Some folks were home. Most were not. Some I knew well. Some hardly at all.

Dad passed away about five months before Christmas. Those five months were hectic. There were legal and banking issues to deal with, his possessions to move and distribute. My home became a storage area for many of his belongings, and was quite cluttered as a result. There were emotions to deal with. Christmas seemed a time to put some closure on a few things, and my yearly Christmas Eve deliveries seemed an appropriate time to wrap up some loose ends.

I ran by my friend Gregg's house and sat for a beer. I went by my friends' Kim and Lisa's homes, too. I met their dogs and their parents. I don't think the dogs or parents cared much for me. Neither Kim nor Lisa ever met my mom, but I know she would have liked them. There were still loads of Mom's stuff in the apartment to go through when Dad passed away. They each got a box of Mom's books.

Dad had specified a Notre Dame pin he wanted to give a friend, Mary Lou. Five months later, on Christmas Eve seemed the time to make a delivery. I enjoyed my surprise visit to her home. I was invited into the home. Her husband said I was going to make her day. I did. Well, Dad did. It kind of felt like that was what Christmas was meant to be.

✧✧✧

Growing up, I remember when Dad got mad he said, "That's sufficient." He said, "If you can't say something nice about someone then don't say anything about them." He liked catsup in the bean soup Mom made. He cut a planter's wart off my foot night after night 'til it was gone. He liked roses and geraniums. He visited his dad on Saturday mornings. He took me shopping one Christmas for presents for Mom. He dropped the new, still in the box, toilet down the steps, and it shattered in a million pieces. He forgot the ham Mom had baked for us to eat for lunch when going to the Indy 500 time trials. He always gave the teachers the benefit of the doubt except one that took a special interest in me and he thought she "was nuts." He said you don't have to agree with a teacher; you just have to give them back the answer they are looking for. He told me I was free to do what I wanted, but there were always consequences for actions. He always purchased a slightly used car. He remembered things. He was a teacher, a boss. He sat at our dining room table working on Social Security disability cases. He drew in an office for me when reviewing designs for the new EAB building. He was not much of a drinker. He headed out to look for me when I was headed in late one evening; I laughed out loud at him. He was wearing an Elmer Fudd hat, had a coiled-up rope over his shoulder, and untied boots on. He took me fishing. He took me hunting. He took me horseback riding. We watched *Hogan's Heroes* regularly. He took me to *007 Live and Let Die* when it was just out at the theatre. Although Mom was gone over five years, he usually wore his wedding ring.

✧ ✧ ✧

I knew when the doctor told Dad he had pancreatic cancer I was going to spend lots of time with him whatever the personal cost. I worried about work, money, and other responsibilities, but I had a deep, peaceful feeling everything would work out fine. When worried, I tried to remind myself of that feeling. I knew Dad's days were numbered, and he was my priority. It came to pass we spent hours a day together, not all day together. We found a level where we were comfortable without ever really discussing it. He needed his time, and I need my time, but we both enjoyed OUR time.

I made a conscious decision not to write anything down about our time together. I knew I wanted to remember the time we spent together, but I didn't want the stress and burden of recording our every move. I needed to be distracted to keep my stress level down, and being worried about writing every day would not accomplish that. What I remember I remember; what is forgotten was not that important, anyway. Looking back, I remember a lot of the last year with my dad. It was a good year. I wouldn't change it. No regrets.

I recall when my parents were dying. They both had cancer. I once told Dad I was pretty screwed because of that! I didn't say it in a mad, mean, or scared way, just being matter of fact. The doctors told Dad what to expect and did not paint a long-term optimistic picture. Mom, on the other hand, had beaten cancer for over five years. She did very well in those five years. Looking back, I'm sure she knew she was dying that last year. I don't know anything about the conversations she had with her doctors, or even if they discussed she could be nearing her end. But I'm pretty sure she knew what was going on inside her. I once told her when we did not ask her questions often and in-depth about her cancer it was not that we did not care; it was just we were scared as hell. She understood.

✦✦✦

I know Dad hid things from me. He hid changes in his body he did not want anyone to know about. He did a good job and could cover for a week or two, but not much longer. His body was shutting down. It could not be hidden long.

Mom did a great job of hiding her body shutting down that last year. I didn't know much about the process of dying until Mom was at VNA. I got on the computer one night and read about the process your body goes through. The entire time I read you could have watched me hitting myself in the head for missing the signs. They were obvious now.

I feel fortunate to have been with both of my parents when they passed away. You get to the point when you know it is time for them to go. You wonder what unfinished business is keeping them here. I'm glad I could be there for them. They went peacefully.

When writing this I jotted the words, "Live Like Frank." I don't think I'll ever really be able to do that. We had different experiences, different influences, different lives, different temperaments. I don't think it's healthy to try and copy him. I can pick some of his good characteristics to incorporate into my life. That's fair and healthy and honorable. I was moving toward a more grateful appreciation of life before Dad got sick. Little things, big things, moments, seconds, actions, scenes, sounds to which we are often blind. Spending seven months with Dad made me many times more appreciative, peaceful, aware, and grateful. It made me more trusting that life will turn out like it should, to go with the flow. It made me much more patient and at peace following my route, not the route imposed on me by others. Dad believed. I can do that.

Dad was a teacher. He taught in his youth in a military school and as a Brother of the Holy Cross, TX. He tried to teach me. I fought, as independent, hard-headed people do. At the end, I did quit fighting and let him teach me some final lessons. Although I must admit that's not why I quit fighting him, and I did not know that's what was happening. I'm glad I got to tell him he was quite the teacher his last six months.

This is the last story I wrote. This is the last story in the book. This is the story that it took me nearly five years to realize needed to be said in print, and not just while talking with friends. This is the story that may be most important to YOU.

I'm a guy posing as a Hemingway. Clearly, I am not a doctor. I am not going to state facts as an attorney might. I do hope you will consider my words. I do hope you will tuck them deep within your head so that they may be recalled if needed. I do hope they ignite your attention should pertinent information cross your path.

This topic is bigger than me. This topic is beyond my knowledge base. This topic is for you to Google. This topic is for you to discuss with your doctor.

For my part I intend to offer but a thought. A thought for you to ponder. A thought that others may not offer. A thought of a potential connection. A thought for you to investigate. A thought better explored earlier than later.

If you or a loved one is diagnosed with diabetes, please consider that diabetes is either a risk factor for, or a symptom of, pancreatic cancer.

✦✦✦

Slowly a man climbed the hill
He was followed,
Sometimes closely, sometimes from afar
The hill was tall, the grade slight, the walk long
The neat grass blew in the light breeze
An occasional tree, a puffy cloud or soaring bird
broke the openness
At the crest stood a stately oak
Its trunk large, leaves many, and shade great
The man sat at the base of the tree
and looked over the quite valley
He was not alone
I was by his side

Acknowledgments

I'd like to take a moment to thank those who may or may not be mentioned by name in this book. My family, lifelong friends, work friends, and all of the more casual acquaintances who played a part in my life during the period of this book.

During the period that Dad was sick and the months following his death I spent hundreds of hours on the phone just talking with friends. Sometimes about important matters and sometimes far from that. I was invited to parties I could not attend. I bounced legal and medical matters off those more knowledgeable and experienced. There were "what if" discussions. There were countless jokes. You called to check in and say hi. You may have even called me when you were having a bad day. You know who you are.

To say I remember all those calls would be a lie. I don't. But the importance of those calls cannot be overstated. After a stressful day of doctor appointments or whatever, an hour on the phone just being "normal" was of great value to me, and therefore Dad, too. Being invited to a party both of us knew I could not attend brought hope for those days to come when I could once again attend.

I'm sorry to say I don't remember everything you did for Dad or me. You sent a text message. You ran an errand. You sat with Dad. You made phone calls. You picked up carryout. You just came and were there if needed. You did so much over such a long period of time.

You offered help. You offered support. You offered a friendly word. You were there when I asked for help.

I thank you. I'm sure Dad does, too.

About the Author

Chris Kern has lived most of his life in Evansville, Indiana. He has traveled throughout the world, from Europe to Central and South America, and throughout the United States.

He received a degree in marketing from the University of Evansville, and much of his career has involved plants: in sales as a wholesale horticulture representative and broker, as well as planting them and photographing them. You have probably seen his photographic work; he has sold thousands of photographs to the nursery industry to be used on plant tags, in catalogs, websites, and even on trucks.

He currently lives on forty acres in southern Indiana with his dog, Kain, where his hobbies are hunting, fishing, and cooking. He has three grown sons and a very new grandson.

You can find out more about him at ChrisKern.com.

www.ingramcontent.com/pod-product-compliance
Lightning Source LLC
LaVergne TN
LVHW041222080426
835508LV00011B/1048